# 100 DREAM CARS

## THE BEST OF *MY RIDE*

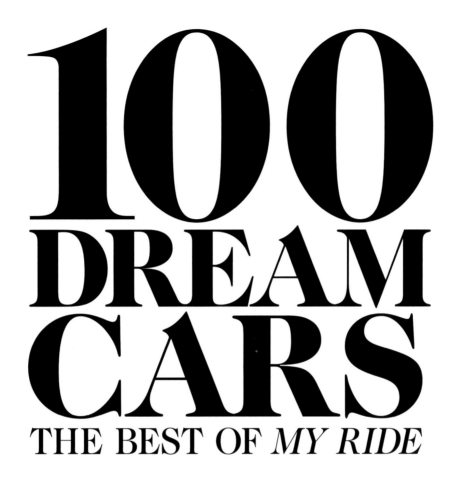

# 100 DREAM CARS

## THE BEST OF *MY RIDE*

BY A.J. BAIME

FOREWORD BY MARIO ANDRETTI

**RIZZOLI** NEW YORK

New York · Paris · London · Milan

# Contents

"To me every hour of the day and night is an unspeakably perfect miracle."
— WALTER CHRYSLER

First published in the United States of America in 2019 by
Rizzoli International Publications, Inc.
300 Park Avenue South
New York, NY 10010
www.rizzoliusa.com

Foreword: Mario Andretti

Page 1: Photography by Ben Sarle
Publisher: Charles Miers
Associate Publisher: James Muschett
Managing Editor: Lynn Scrabis
Editor: Elizabeth Smith
Art Direction: Edward Leida
Design: Sherry Wang
Photo Editor: Leah Latella

Printed in China

2020 2021 2022 2023 / 10 9 8 7 6 5 4 3 2

ISBN: 978-8478-6623-6
Library of Congress Control Number: 2019936870

Visit us online:
Facebook.com/RizzoliNewYork
Twitter: @Rizzoli_Books
Instagram.com/RizzoliBooks
Pinterest.com/RizzoliBooks
Youtube.com/user/RizzoliNY
Issuu.com/Rizzoli

# Foreword by
## Mario Andretti

**WHEN I WAS GROWING UP IN ITALY**, in the years after World War II, my family lived for a time in a refugee camp in the city of Lucca. It was a medieval town, a labyrinth surrounded by a city wall, and right across from where we lived was a parking garage. Parking was at a premium because Lucca was built hundreds of years before cars existed.

My twin brother, Aldo, and I spent all our time at this garage, talking about racing with the guys who worked there, and at age eleven, we started parking cars—little Fiat Topolinos. By the time we were fourteen, we were parking Alfa Romeos and doing burnouts. When my family crossed the ocean and settled in Nazareth, Pennsylvania, in 1955, I knew how to handle a car. My father bought a Ford and my brother and I went everywhere flat out in that thing. I flipped it a couple times—the last time for good.

People sometimes ask me if I had a "eureka" moment, when I knew that driving cars would be my future. I did. I've had a passion for racing since I can remember—I don't know why—and one day in the spring of 1963, when I was twenty-three, I won three feature races in midget cars in two different towns. At the time, the dean of motorsport writers was named Chris Economaki. He was announcing the last race I won that day, in Hatfield, Pennsylvania. His voice was shrill over the loudspeaker. He said, "Mario, you have just won a ticket to the big time!" I can still hear his voice now. That moment will stay with me forever.

Throughout my career, every time I've gotten into a car—whether I was winning the Indy 500 or the Formula 1 world championship—I've had to be able to wring everything I could out of the machine. When you are motoring at over two hundred miles per hour with a cement wall an inch away on one side and another car an inch away on the other, it is life or death. You have to have confidence in the car. You have to find that feel. The feeling is something almost impossible to describe. You feel how the car responds to your command, so you have the confidence to push harder, to go faster and farther.

What do I drive now? I have a 2018 Lamborghini Aventador S, a 2019 Corvette ZR1, and a 2016 Jaguar XJL. There's a new Lincoln Navigator in my garage as well as a new Mini Cooper, and I keep an Audi Q7 at my home in Florida. Finally, there's an old Ford Bronco that belonged to my father, with only forty thousand miles on it.

I love all of these cars. They have meaning for me beyond their simple purpose of transportation, and that is what this whole book is about—how a car can be so much more than the sum of its parts. Having spent a lifetime at the wheel, I have been blessed to drive some fine vehicles in my time. I wish I had room in my garage for all of them.

# The Biggest, Baddest Car that Could Exist

*Photography by Jason Keen*

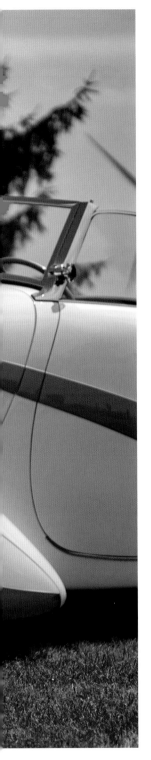

**IT WAS THE SUMMER OF 2013,** and the phone rang in my office. An editor I had worked with named Adam Thompson at the *The Wall Street Journal* wanted to know if I would put together a pitch for a new kind of car column, about people who own cool vehicles. I thought: That's a terrible idea. Then I thought: Actually, it's genius.

For over five years and running, every week, the My Ride column has appeared in the *WSJ*. Each week there is a profile of a person who has an extraordinary story about a vehicle he or she owns. *The Wall Street Journal's* Life & Arts photo team dispatches top photographers all over the country to shoot these stories, and sometimes abroad. That effort is led by photo editor Leah Latella, who also did the photo editing of this book in a freelance capacity. There's the pizza delivery man who dodges polar bears in his Hyundai in the northernmost town in the United States. The comedian with his real-life Batmobile. The Connecticut IT professional who races her 180 miles per hour Ferrari on weekends. The retired entrepreneur in Kentucky with his twenty-two-foot-long 1937 Cadillac, which he calls "the biggest, baddest car that could exist."

Each of these stories is an "as told to" interview. I interview the subject by phone and write the story in his or her words, then we fact check it together. The best part about the process is the pleasure it brings to the subject of the story. In a world that feels so full of conflict, these stories are mood adjusters.

What's the point, in the end? Now as much as ever, the love between "man and machine" continues to burn. Sometimes the relationship between people and their cars (or motorcycles or monster trucks or even military tanks and amphibious vehicles) can tell us volumes about the human condition.

Today, we are on the threshold of a new automotive black swan moment. For the first time since Henry Ford's Model T revolutionized society over a century ago, engineers and entrepreneurs are reinventing the wheel—changing the way we move around our cities and towns, even the way we look and think of cars in the first place. Electric autonomous vehicles are already cruising our roads in vast numbers, and soon enough, our pizzas will be delivered by rolling ATM machines powered by big batteries and artificial intelligence.

What better time to capture the romance between humans and their steering wheels? To explore the horsepower of today and the internal combustion engines of the past? Let's hit the road . . .

# Thunderbirds Don't Get More Fabulous Than This

**Merle Mullin, an artist/designer from Los Angeles, CA, and her 1957 Ford Thunderbird**

**ON THE OCCASION** of my first anniversary with my husband Peter, in 2001, we had dinner at the Hotel Bel-Air. After, I asked the valet for my BMW station wagon. He returned with this beautiful white Thunderbird. I said, "This is not my car." My husband said, "I guess you'd better get in and drive it home."

I figured out quickly: This was not a joke. I had owned a 1957 T-Bird years earlier, and I had often said to my husband, "I wish I had never sold that car. How did I not know it would become such a classic?"

He had made a lot of phone calls to find out what color my old T-Bird was, and what model year, and he had purchased this car for me. I was stunned to the bottom of my feet.

The T-Bird is an icon. Ford first introduced the car for model year 1955, and along with the Corvette, it is considered to be one of the first American sports cars. Ford was known at the time for more staid, functional cars, so this was an anomaly, and very few from this era were built.

My husband and I redid the suspension, so the car drives very smoothly. I love the simplicity. When you look at the dashboard and then you look at the dashboard of, say, a Tesla, the difference is remarkable.

Later this summer, I will be driving this car—which turns sixty this year—in a rally called It's All About the Girls! Women from seven countries, with their cars, will meet in Les Baux-de-Provence, France. We will spend five days on driving excursions, for fun and to raise money for charities.

I became a car girl by osmosis, as I am surrounded by car talk. [A.J.: Ms. Mullin's husband Peter is the founder of the Mullin Automotive Museum in Oxnard, California, and chairman of the board of the Petersen Automotive Museum in Los Angeles.] I have been fortunate enough to drive wonderful cars, but the T-Bird is extra special. All my passion for motoring, for my husband, and for my memories of youth are embodied in this one car.

*Photography by Emily Berl*

SPECS

Merle Mullin's 1957 Ford Thunderbird

Engine: 312 cc, V-8

Top Speed: 117 mph

Tires: American Classic

Details of Merle Mullin's 1957 Ford Thunderbird.
The car was a gift to her from her husband Peter,
who is a well-known figure in the car world.

All my passion for motoring, for my
husband, and for my memories of
youth are embodied in this one car.

# One Million Miles in a 1964 Porsche 356C

## Guy Newmark, a yacht broker and marina owner from San Pedro, CA

OF ALL THE BIRTHDAY PARTIES I have been to, none was more fun than the fifty-second birthday party for my car last October. I set up the party at a brewery near me. I timed it so that, the moment I drove in, the odometer would flip. All the nines would turn to zeros as the car hit its one millionth mile.

My father gave the 356 to me when I graduated the University of California at Berkeley in the 1960s. I had a big smile on my face that day, and I'm still smiling. I named the car Blu, thinking that was the German spelling for blue; I was wrong, but the name stuck.

The 356—Porsche's first production model, introduced in 1948—is the car that put the brand on the map. This one already had about 78,000 miles on it when I got it. As a yacht broker, I was required to show boats all over California and to drive to far-flung places to get signatures on contracts. Some years, Blu and I drove over 30,000 miles.

The car only broke down once, and it was easily fixed. Almost everything is original, though I have repainted it and rebuilt the engine twice.

Not long before the car's birthday party last October, Blu got stolen out of my garage. Almost instantly, I had Porsche fans all over California looking for it. A woman not far from where I live called saying there was a blue Porsche parked in front of her house, and indeed, it was my car. I paid her a nice reward.

When the day came for Blu's party and its millionth mile, a film crew was in town from Germany to capture the moment, so we were able to film the odometer flipping from nines to zeros as I pulled up to the brewery. There was a 1960s band playing, and since it was October and the car is German, we had an Oktoberfest theme. Beers for everyone. It was a terrific time.

Since then, I've put another two thousand miles on the car—just a few more to go until two million.

**SPECS**

Guy Newmark's 1964 Porsche 356C

Engine: 1600 cc, boxer 4-cylinder

Top Speed: About 110 mph

Tires: Dunlop

*Photography by Joseph Philipson*

# A Ferrari Saleswoman's
# Thirty-Five-Miles-Per-Hour Escape

### Colleen Sheehan, a saleswoman with Ferraris Online from Costa Mesa, CA, and her 1930 BMW 3/15 DA2 Cabriolet

IN 2000, when I was eight years old, my father took possession of the BMW you see here as part of a business deal. The car had belonged to the owner of a famous fast-food chain, and my father thought it would be cute to give it to my twin brother Mick and I. With a lot of help from my dad, we fixed the car up.

In 2003, we took it to the Pebble Beach Concours d'Elegance (the most prestigious classic car show in the country). It placed third in its class, and at eleven years old, I became one of the youngest people ever to drive onto the Pebble Beach Concours podium. That ignited a motoring passion that has never left me.

BMW was founded in 1916 as an airplane engine manufacturer in Germany. The company started building motorcycles during the 1920s and completed its first car in 1929. We believe our 1930 car is the oldest original-bodied BMW in this country. We have taken the vehicle to numerous car shows and BMW events, and we have never found or heard of an older BMW with its original body in the U.S.

These cars are rare today because so many were destroyed during World War II. The story we have been told is that our car was used by German doctors during the war, and it survived. At some point, it found its way to the U.S.

As a Ferrari salesperson, I am often driving cars that can shoot past one hundred miles per hour with ease. Driving a 1930 BMW is even more thrilling because it is such a change of pace. The car has a roughly 750-cubic-centimeter four-cylinder, with three speeds and fifteen horsepower. (That's where the 3/15 in the name comes from.)

Top speed is thirty-five miles per hour, and that's if you're going downhill with a tailwind. Due to the 1930 suspension and steering, keeping the car in its lane is a mission in itself. Every bump moves the car, so you sort of bounce down the road.

My favorite thing to do with the BMW is to take it to brunch on a weekend and sit outside, so I can watch the reactions people have when they see it. It sparks joy and curiosity everywhere it goes.

## The story we have been told is that our car was used by German doctors during the war, and it survived.

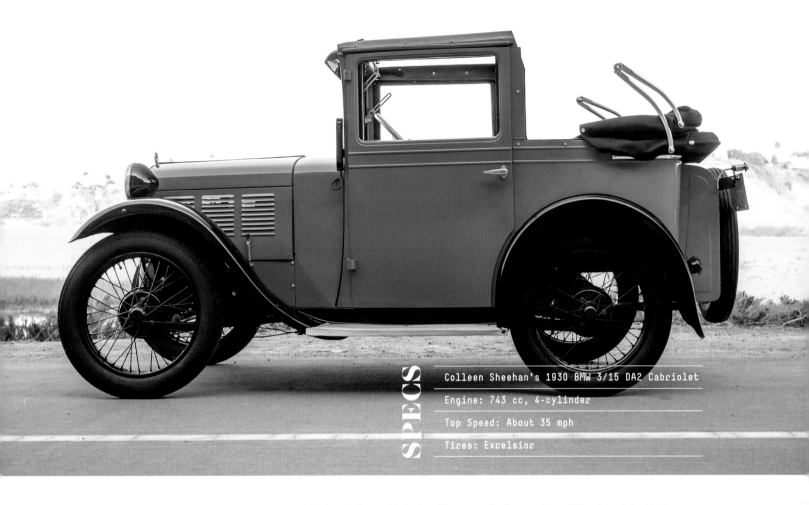

SPECS

Colleen Sheehan's 1930 BMW 3/15 DA2 Cabriolet

Engine: 743 cc, 4-cylinder

Top Speed: About 35 mph

Tires: Excelsior

Colleen Sheehan's 1930 BMW 3/15 DA2. Ms. Sheehan believes this is the oldest BMW in the U.S. that still has its original body.

# The Serious Hot-Rodder's Model of Choice: A 1932 Ford Hot Rod

## Paul Waller, thirty-five, a Fender master guitar builder from Temecula, CA

THE HOT-ROD phenomenon began in the late 1920s. Young guys would find junkyard cars, put a big motor in them, and race around the streets. A whole new era was born. The 1932 Ford introduced the highly modifiable and affordable flathead V-8, and it became the hot-rodder's model of choice.

My father started building my 1932 Ford three-window coupe, but he never finished it. We made a deal and I took it over. In my line of work, there's tons of sanding, shaping, and prepping for paint, and I used that same approach.

I built the car to look like something out of the late 1950s, with skinny tires and a chopped roof. The paint job took six months; I had to take the car apart—every nut, every bolt. I used the same urethane, called demon black, that we spray on the black Fender Stratocasters built in the U.S. factory.

My father had pulled a 327 Chevrolet engine out of an old El Camino, and so the car's drivetrain is Chevy. I get about twenty miles per gallon—not bad for a carbureted old motor.

Weather permitting, I drive the car to work most of the week. While it has updated brakes and three-point-harness seat belts, it's not exactly ergonomic. And the suspension technology is eighty years old, so the car handles like a school bus on peanut butter in turns. But in a straight line doing 80 miles per hour? It's just a different kind of fun.

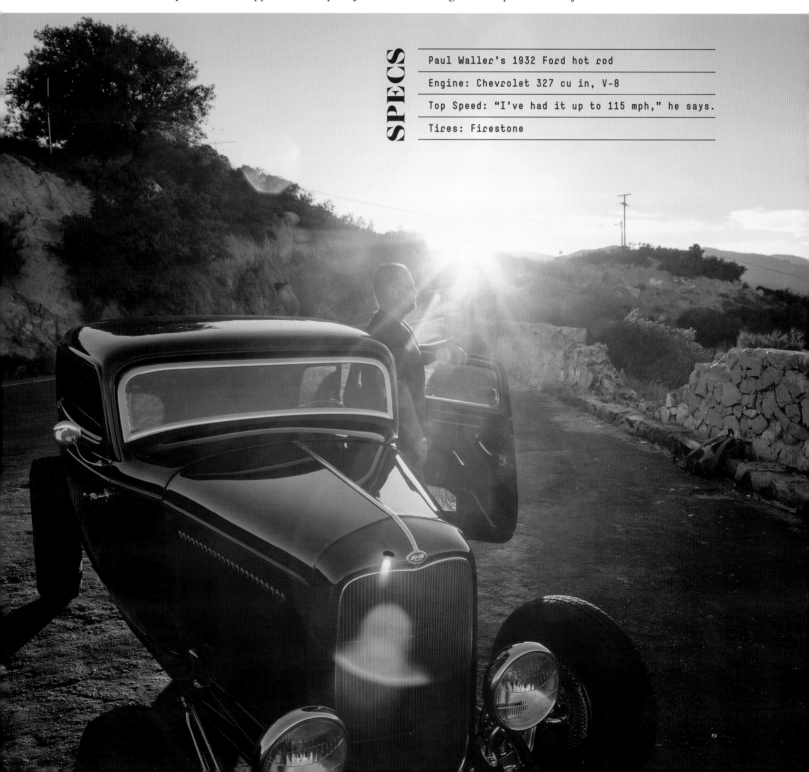

**SPECS**

Paul Waller's 1932 Ford hot rod

Engine: Chevrolet 327 cu in, V-8

Top Speed: "I've had it up to 115 mph," he says.

Tires: Firestone

## Rock and Rolling
**In no particular order, master guitar builder Paul Waller picks his top-ten bands for long-distance drives**

1. Rolling Stones
2. Led Zeppelin
3. Beatles
4. Metallica
5. Primus
6. Tom Waits
7. Tom Petty
8. Modest Mouse
9. Howlin' Wolf
10. Tool

**The 1932 Ford introduced the highly modifiable and affordable Flathead V-8, and it became the hot-rodder's model of choice.**

SPECS

Jeff Zischke's 1991 Nissan Figaro

Engine: 1.0 L, turbo 4-cylinder

Top Speed: About 95 mph

Tires: Kelly

# How a 1991 Nissan Figaro Became an Instant Classic in the U.S.

### Jeff Zischke, sixty-one, an artist and designer from Scottsdale, AZ

**AS AN ARTIST** and a car fan, I'm always looking for vehicles with sensual shapes and unique color combinations. I've sought out interesting cars and motorcycles all my life, but none can top the Figaro.

Only twenty thousand were sold, all in one year—1991. The two-seater caused a craze in Japan, mostly because of its cartoonish styling cues. But Nissan never exported any. Over the years, the Figaro gained a cult following in some other countries, but never here, because, according to law, you cannot bring a car into the U.S. if it was not officially imported until the car is twenty-five years old—at which point it's deemed a classic, which means it's exempt from government emissions and safety standards.

I first saw a Figaro online and I was instantly intrigued. Two years ago, I was in Vancouver walking in the rain when I saw one parked on the side of the road. I thought: Oh my God, I want that car! So I went on a quest.

Canada doesn't have the same laws as the States, so I was able to locate a few in the Vancouver area. All were in bad shape, except one. The owner loved the car (her license plate read FIGGY), so it took some convincing. I got the car for what I thought was a good price.

Still, I had to wait eleven months before the car turned twenty-five and I could bring it across the border. I kept it at a friend's place in Vancouver, and twice I went up to drive it. This was nerve-racking because it's right-hand drive (they drive on the left side of the road in Japan), and I didn't know my way around in Canada.

I took the car home the first week of January in 2016, and while I can't prove it, I'm pretty sure it was the first one legally brought into the U.S. as a classic. I put my own vanity plate on: GROOVN. The car relates so well to my lifestyle, because it's like a piece of sculpture. All the signage is in Japanese, and it has these little Figaro design elements all over it.

People go crazy because they've never seen anything like it. When I drive it, I bring smiles to the world.

**Artist Jeff Zischke and his Nissan Figaro. Only twenty thousand of these cars were sold, all built in Japan in 1991. Mr. Zischke believes his is the first imported legally into the U.S.**

**People go crazy because they've never seen anything like it. When I drive it, I bring smiles to the world.**

# A British Land Rover for the All-American Road Trip

**Blake Hennessy, thirty-two, an employment consultant from Burr Ridge, IL, and his 1989 Land Rover Defender 110**

**AT FIRST, WE WERE** planning on driving to a trade show in Arizona. But then we thought, if we're going that far, why not make it a big trip and cross some things off the bucket list? It was late spring, the beginning of road-trip season. My childhood buddy Rob Bedoe and I cleared thirty days and mapped out ten thousand miles, down to Texas, over to the West Coast, to the Canadian border and back.

I'd found the Land Rover online eighteen months earlier. It was in Lakeland, Florida, and the price was so good, I would have been a fool not to buy it. I flew down there, paid in cash, and drove it home. Defenders are four-wheel-drive go-anywhere, do-anything vehicles. Land Rover built these trucks for over sixty-eight years. You don't have to worry about road conditions or the weather. You just keep on going.

We left on a Friday. I've driven a lot of crazy cars, and I can say that this one gets a lot of attention because it looks like something out of Jurassic Park. The truck was originally purchased in the U.K., so it's right-hand drive. The old V-8 eats a lot of oil and gas. If I was averaging eleven miles per gallon (pretty terrible), I wasn't complaining. We did hit some weather. There's a lot of water ingress with this truck, but that's part of its charisma.

For a tent, I went with a company called Tepui. They make tents that mount on top of your vehicle, and even in bad weather, it didn't leak once. The tent and awning take five minutes to put up and five minutes to take down.

We saw amazing things. The waterfalls at Yosemite were in full force. The wildlife in Yellowstone was like nothing I'd ever seen. I remember this duck chili at Yaks in the middle of nowhere—Dunsmuir, California— and the fried chicken at Swift Lounge in Portland, Oregon.

When I bought the Land Rover, I was thinking I'd drive it for a while and sell it for profit, but I've grown attached to it now. Next up: From Canada's east coast to the Florida Keys.

*Photography by Clayton Hauck*

SPECS

Blake Hennessy's 1989 Land Rover Defender 110

Engine: 3.5 L, V-8

Top Speed: About 85 mph

Tires: Kenda

## The World According to Blake
**A lifelong wheel nut, Mr. Hennessy picks the top-ten most beautiful cars of all time.**

1. 1935 Voisin C28 Aérosport
2. 1937 Talbot-Lago T150-C SS
3. 1954 Porsche 550 Glöckler Spyder
4. 1955 Mercedes-Benz 300 SLR Coupe
5. 1957 Volvo Sugga TP21
6. 1965 Lincoln Continental Convertible
7. 1970 Plymouth Hemi Cuda
8. 1996 Ferrari F50 GT
9. 2010 Koenigsegg CCXR Special Edition
10. 2016 Land Rover Defender 110

# Can't Afford a Shelby?
# Just Build Your Own

### Paul Martin, a Los Angeles commercial set designer and his 1964 Shelby Cobra Daytona Coupe Re-creation

IN THE EARLY 1960S, a car designer named Peter Brock, working for Carroll Shelby's Shelby American racing team, designed the Shelby Cobra Daytona Coupe. It became the first car from an American team to win the 24 Hours of Le Mans in its class, and a year later, it was part of the Shelby American team that won the FIA world championship. Only six were built. Today, they are among the most sought-after collector cars in the world.

Since I did not have the millions it would take to buy one, I decided to build my own. My wife and my friends thought I was mad, which is probably true. Three and a half years ago, I set out to build an exact re-creation of the 1964 car.

For the chassis and body, I hired craftsmen in Poland who work at a former MiG jet fighter factory there. They spent some three thousand hours on the project, working from original drawings and photographs. Meanwhile, I found parts all over the U.S. and Europe. If I could not find the exact part I needed, I had it fabricated.

I had a period-correct 289 Ford racing engine built. The brake cooling ducts, the four-speed transmission, Weber carburetors—everything had to match the original car, down to the dashboard switches and even the style of lettering above them. The major difference between the old and new car? Mine is street legal.

Part of the fun was documenting this on Facebook. Throughout, I posted photographs of the progress. By the end, I had tons of people following the journey.

When I completed the car in 2016, members of a Shelby club threw an unveiling party in Beverly Hills. Special guests included the Cobra Daytona Coupe's original designer, Peter Brock, who signed the dashboard, and Allen Grant, a racing driver who competed in the original car in the 1960s. It was truly incredible.

The vehicle probably cost me a half-million dollars. I drive it to events, to the beach and through the mountains. It's a raw race car for the street, capable of 200 mph. Sitting in it with the engine revving, you feel like you're inside a snare drum. It's that loud. My wife calls it noisy, scary, dirty, and frightening. I call it a work of art.

*Photography by David Walter Banks*

**SPECS**

Paul Martin's 1964 Shelby Cobra Daytona Coupe Re-creation

Engine: Ford 289 cu in, V-8

Top Speed: "I think 200 mph," says Martin.

Tires: Firestone racing

# It's that loud. My wife calls it noisy, scary, dirty, and frightening. I call it a work of art.

Paul Martin and the 1964 Shelby Cobra Daytona Coupe re-creation. With a lot of help
and a lot of money, Mr. Martin built this car from the ground up.

# That's Amour: Falling for a 1986 Citroën Deux Chevaux

## Veronica DeGuenther, sixty-nine, a medical-malpractice insurance saleswoman from Tampa, FL

**WHEN I WAS A KID,** I went everywhere with my dad and when he worked on cars, I would hand him the tools. It fascinated me to learn what makes wheels go around. When I got my license, my parents gave me a broken-down 1959 Ford Anglia, made in England. My dad said, "You know how to fix it." I still have scratches on my high school ring from tearing down that engine.

Today, I have two collector cars that could not be more disparate. One is a 1999 Porsche 911 I named Killer Bee because it has a black leather interior and Speed Yellow paint. I drove that car on the racetrack at Le Mans in France. She recently turned her 105,000th mile doing switchbacks in the North Carolina mountains.

My other car is a 1986 Citroën 2CV, or Deux Chevaux. In 2007, I told a friend who lives in Europe that I was looking for a car I could show at car shows and just have fun with. He emailed me pictures of this car, and I fell in love with it instantly. I bought it and had it shipped to Florida. A friend came up with a name: Beestro. [A.J.: A play on bistro and Ms. DeGuenther's other car, Killer Bee.]

First built in 1948, Deux Chevaux means "two horses". [A.J.: Referring to a horsepower taxation classification] In Europe, this car is an icon. Millions were made over forty-two years, for people who could not afford nicer cars.

The seats and doors detach easily, so—as lore has it—farmers could stuff these cars with goats, eggs, and vegetables, drive to market, unload, hose out the car, then put the seats back in so they could drive their families to church on Sunday.

When I bought my Deux Chevaux, I also bought a trailer to tow it, and I have had Beestro at car shows in Florida, Kentucky, North Carolina, New Jersey, and New York. The night before I go to a show, I order fresh baguettes from a local grocery store. I pick them up in the morning so the car smells like a French bakery, then I hand out baguettes to the friends I make.

I also drive this car around where I live as much as possible. Valet parkers at my favorite restaurants always park her right in front. Like Killer Bee, Beestro gets lots of attention.

## My dad said, "You know how to fix it." I still have scratches on my high school ring from tearing down that engine.

*Photography by Bob Croslin*

**DOLLY**

**976 QY 28**

**SPECS**

Veronica DeGuenther's Citroën Deux Chevaux

Engine: 602 cc, boxer 4-cylinder

Top Speed: About 85 mph

Tires: Michelin

**SPECS**

| | |
|---|---|
| The Norwood Family's 1978 GMC Jimmy | |
| Engine: 350 cu in, V-8 | |
| Top speed: 117 mph | |
| Tires: BF Goodrich | |

# To Alaska, Back, and Beyond for a 1978 GMC Jimmy

## Three generations of the Norwood family from Midland, TX

**FRANK NORWOOD, eighty-nine, a retired insurance agent:** In 1978, I bought the Jimmy new for about $7,500. I could not imagine that nearly forty years later, our family would still own this vehicle, and I would have such a story to tell.

The Jimmy started out as a work truck. I used it to build a log cabin in New Mexico. I made about 125 round trips over three years, over five hundred miles each, hauling everything from logs to furniture, sometimes thousands of pounds on a trailer. That log cabin is still in our family. Eventually, my son John was driving the Jimmy to Midland High School. We drove the Jimmy on family trips to Alaska, through British Columbia, the Yukon, and the Northwest Territories. We took it to Wyoming, and to Battle Creek, Michigan—my wife, the grandchildren, a dog, and I.

In 2010, I decided to sell the Jimmy. I asked my son John if he wanted it, and he said no.

**JOHN NORWOOD, fifty-one, an oil and gas investor:** I was in the seventh grade when my dad bought that truck. After two years of it being gone from the family, I found the new owner and bought it back. The Jimmy underwent a yearlong restoration. The engine is original and has about 250,000 miles on it. (The odometer broke for some time, so we can't be sure.) You can imagine how proud my wife D'Ann and I were when we gave the truck to our son, Andrew, so he could drive it to Midland High, just like I did.

**ANDREW NORWOOD, twenty, a University of Oklahoma student:** The first time I drove the Jimmy to school, all my friends came around to see it. I had teachers saying, "I had a truck like that when I was young. If you ever think of selling it . . ." For a while, the horn would go off every time I made a left turn. I figured out how to go places so I only had to make right turns. The gauges didn't always work, and once I ran out of gas.

My younger brother Philip just got his driver's license, and in the fall, he will drive the Jimmy to high school. The Jimmy is like a brother. You get mad at it, you argue with it, but at the end of the day, you love it.

**The Norwood family with their 1978 GMC Jimmy, which has been in the family for generations.
One photograph to the right shows the vehicle pulling construction wood, many years ago.**

SPECS

| Heidi Lynn Ferguson's 1969 Cadillac DeVille |
| --- |
| Engine: 472 cu in, V-8 |
| Top Speed: About 85 mph |
| Tires: Vogue |

**Heidi Lynn Ferguson with her two Cadillacs. She admits that, when she drops her kids off at school in a Caddy with bullhorns on the nose, they get a little embarrassed.**

SPECS

| 1976 Cadillac Eldorado |
| --- |
| Engine: 500 cu in, V-8 |
| Top Speed: About 85 mph |
| Tires: Hankook |

# 1969 Cadillac DeVille /
# 1976 Cadillac Eldorado:
## A Pair of Cruisers

**Heidi Lynn Ferguson, forty, a corporate flight attendant from West Palm Beach, FL**

EVERY WEEKDAY, all over the country, communities participate in a ritual: dropping off kids at school. When I was a girl, my family moved from a farm in Oregon into an upper-crust neighborhood in Portland. There was nowhere to put the livestock, so there was always animals in the back of our truck when my dad dropped me off at school. (I don't think he ever even came to a full stop.) I was so embarrassed, and I promised I'd never do that to my kids. I guess I was wrong.

I have two old Cadillacs. In 2013, I bought a 1969 DeVille for $500. It wasn't running, but all the parts were there, and I did all the work myself except the brakes and the paint. I YouTubed stuff, read a lot online, and figured out how to get the car running through trial and error. Then I put the decal on it—a skull and crossbones on the hood.

A year later, a friend tipped me off about another Cadillac—a 1976 Eldorado—for sale in a condo complex. As soon as I saw the thing, I had a vision for it. The car wasn't running, and the hood and trunk-lid were rusted out. It had ninety thousand miles on it. I bought it for $1,000, then I went shopping: at a junkyard for parts, and an antiques show for the horns. I grew up a huge Dukes of Hazzard fan, so I built my own Boss Hogg Cadillac.

I love these cars. They're American made, and the engines are original. They're great expressions of my personality: I'm a little bit country, a little rock 'n' roll.

I have two kids now about the same age I was when my dad used to drop me off at school in the old farm truck. When I drop my kids off in one of the Cadillacs, the car gets a lot of attention. The parents and teachers think it's hilarious, but my kids get a little embarrassed, especially when the 1969 DeVille backfires. There's no livestock in the back of these cars. But I guess that can be arranged.

## I love these cars . . . They're great expressions of my personality: I'm a little bit country, a little rock 'n' roll.

# An All-Original 1970 Pontiac GTO Judge Is a Rare Find

## Wade Kawasaki, fifty-six, president and chief operating officer of the Coker Group of automotive companies, based in Chattanooga, TN

**GROWING UP,** I worked at my father's Shell station in downtown L.A. I would wash windows and check oil, and I got my hands on all these amazing cars in the early 1970s, from Corvettes to Camaros. I had a love affair in particular with the Pontiac GTO Judge.

Fast-forward decades later. It's 2014, and I was on vacation in Hawaii, visiting a grade-school friend. He had purchased an old muscle car, aiming to restore it, but he couldn't find the time. Would I be interested in buying it?

People talk about "barn finds," beat-up old cars found in barns, that turn out to be gemlike automobiles in need of restoration. This car was not in a barn; it was in a garage. But it was the same experience. When my son Timothy and I looked at the car, we realized we had found an amazing GTO Judge.

It had a couple dents and had some primer on it, but the original paint was underneath. The V-8 engine, the transmission, even the water pump—everything was original, and all the documentation was there. The first owner had lived

Wade Kawasaki first fell in love with the Pontiac GTO Judge when he was a kid working on cars at his father's gas station. This car he found in Hawaii.

*Photography by David Walter Banks*

**SPECS**

Wade Kawasaki's 1969 Pontiac GTO Judge

Engine: 400 cu in, V-8

Top Speed: 125 mph

Tires: Firestone

Some of the restoration of Wade Kawasaki's 1970 Pontiac GTO Judge was documented on the television show *American Restoration*. When Mr. Kawasaki found the car, it only had forty-eight thousand miles on it.

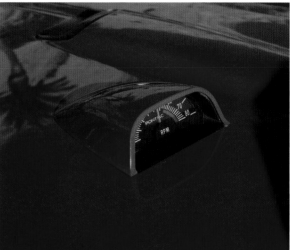

in Maui; there are not a lot of roads on the island, so the Judge only had 48,000 miles on it.

Pontiac first debuted its GTO in 1964, the same year the Ford Mustang appeared. In fact, many call the GTO the very first muscle car. The Judge was a special GTO first unleashed in 1969. It is known for its rear wing and its high performance, and it was reputedly named for the famous Sammy Davis Jr. TV skit "Here Comes the Judge."

I bought the car and had it shipped to Los Angeles. When I picked it up, amazingly, the engine started, and I drove it to our family home in Palos Verdes. Some of the restoration was documented on the TV show *American Restoration*, and the 100 percent–finished car made its debut at the SEMA trade show in Las Vegas in 2015. [A.J.: Mr. Kawasaki is chairman of the board of directors of SEMA, the Specialty Equipment Market Association.]

It has been a dream come true to reconnect with this old friend, a dream car from my youth.

# Pontiac first debuted its GTO in 1964, the same year the Ford Mustang appeared. In fact, many call the GTO the very first muscle car.

Iron Maiden drummer Nicko McBrain shows off "Priscilla," his customized 2013 Jaguar XKR-S.
The car has signage written in the classic Iron Maiden font.

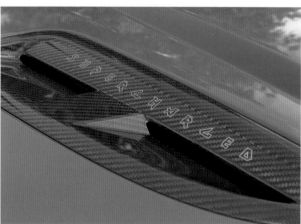

On Iron Maiden's mid-'80s World Slavery Tour, the whole band rented Jaguar XJ6s. There were five of us at the time, driving these cars across Britain.

*Photography by Josh Ritchie*

# Meet "Priscilla": Iron Maiden Drummer's Custom Jag

**Nicko McBrain, a hard rock drummer based in Boca Raton, FL,
and his 2013 Jaguar XKR-S**

**I WAS TEN YEARS OLD**, walking down a street in North London with my dad, when we saw a Jaguar Mark X pass by. I'll never forget it. My dad turned and said, "That is the most beautiful car. I'm going to own one someday." When I started making money in the 1980s, I wanted to buy him a Mark X, but I lost him in 1985. He never did get to own one.

Around the time he passed away, I started driving these cars myself. On Iron Maiden's mid-'80s World Slavery Tour, the whole band rented Jaguar XJ6s. There were five of us at the time, driving these cars across Britain. Two years later, I bought my first Jaguar (also an XJ6). Now I have four "cats" in my garage, and my daily driver is Priscilla (my wife Rebecca came up with the name), an XKR-S customized at the factory in England.

I had the Jaguar Growler logo made to look like Eddie, the Iron Maiden mascot, on the center wheel caps, the grille of the car, and embroidered on the seat backs. The writing on the car is done in Iron Maiden font—the word "supercharged" on the hood, the "Jaguar" on the wheels, and on the running board it says "Nicko McBrain XKR-S."

The glove box is done in piano-black lacquer, and on it is written the words "Made In Aluminium," with the extra i, the correct way of spelling the word [as it is spelled in Britain]. The car is the only XKR-S in the world with this color, Ultra Blue. At the time it was built, the supercharged 5.0-liter V-8 was the most powerful production Jaguar engine ever (550 horsepower). All in, I paid about $150,000. I got a VIP deal on the custom work.

Just last week, we got a new cat in the litter. I bought my wife a new Jaguar F-Type R. That car has basically the same engine as Priscilla, but it's a lighter vehicle, so that means it's the fastest pussycat in my garage.

I'm not so much a petrol head that I know the torque values on all kinds of cars. I'm just a Jag nut. That's me.

**SPECS**

| | |
|---|---|
| Nicko McBrain's Iron Maiden Jaguar 2013 XKR-S | |
| Engine: 5 L, V-8 | |
| Top Speed: About 180 mph | |
| Tires: Pirelli | |

# It's Her Thing:
# A Strange 1973 Volkswagen

**Brenda Berys, director of events at Gigya, a tech company, based in San Francisco, CA**

YOU NEVER KNOW when a chance encounter is going to change your life. In 2006, I was walking through a parking lot in Miami when I saw this bright yellow car. I was immediately struck by it. By the end of that day, I had found the owner, who was this beautiful, eccentric blond woman. I said, "I want that car." She said, "Whoa! Settle down." We started talking, and we became instant friends.

Four years later, we both moved to the West Coast, and had the Thing shipped to East Palo Alto. We had the engine rebuilt, banged out all the dents, and got to work, hoping we could blaze future careers in the nonprofit world. We drove that car all over—a blonde and a redhead, sun shining, no roof. Friends started calling us "The Girls in the Car." To us, the Thing represented our new lives and all the good we were going to do for people.

For the few who recognized the car, it brought back all these memories of the 1970s. The Thing was a descendant of a German World War II vehicle, and it was only sold in the U.S. for about two years starting in 1973. The doors are detachable, the windshield folds down, and the car supposedly could float. It's not quite a dune buggy, not quite a Jeep. It's just . . . a Thing. It remains one of the most unusual cars ever to roll down a road.

Soon after the Thing appeared in 1973, the federal government and Ralph Nader criticized it for not meeting safety standards. After just two years, sales ended in the U.S.

About five years ago, my friend moved away, but she left the Thing for me. Driving it is still so much fun. It feels like a go-kart on the road, and everywhere I go, VW enthusiasts come out of the woodwork to share their car stories with me. The Thing lacks every comfort and convenience, and it's broken down a million times. But still, its charm never wears thin.

**Brenda Berys calls her 1973 Volkswagen Thing "one of the most unusual cars ever to roll down a road."
VW sold the Thing for only about two years in the U.S., starting in 1973.**

SPECS

Brenda Berys's 1973 Volkswagen Thing

Engine: 1600 cc, 4-cylinder

Top speed: About 85 mph (downhill!)

Tires: Primewell

# The Thing lacks every comfort and convenience, and it's broken down a million times. But still, its charm never wears thin.

# Back to the Future in His 1981 DeLorean DMC-12

## Ronald Ferguson, engineer and president of the DeLorean Owners Association

MY FATHER AND I always considered the DeLorean special. The car was immortalized in Back to the Future, a movie we saw in the theater together. One day in 2000, I had the idea to buy a DeLorean for him. I paid $15,000. (It needed some work.) We joined a local club and attended DeLorean conventions as far off as Europe. My dad is gone now, but the car has stayed with me.

When I drive it, people are always snapping pictures, and police have stopped me to get a closer look. Usually there's a long delay before I can leave a gas station. The car has been the centerpiece of weddings, cross-country rallies, and fundraisers.

The DeLorean's story is one that Hollywood could never create. It begins with John DeLorean, a maverick who abandoned what was certainly a path to the presidency of General Motors to start his own car company. Along the way, we meet investors like Johnny Carson and Sammy Davis Jr., and later infamous characters in an FBI sting. [A.J.: A jury acquitted Mr. DeLorean of cocaine charges on the basis of entrapment in 1984.]

The DMC-12 was only in production from 1981 to 1982. The experiment ultimately failed, but with its gull-wing doors and brushed stainless-steel body panels, the car will always remain ahead of its time.

**The experiment ultimately failed, but with its gull-wing doors and brushed stainless-steel body panels, the car will always remain ahead of its time.**

Ronald Ferguson, a fan of the movie *Back to the Future*, with his DeLorean DMC-12.
The car was only in production in 1981 and 1982, but it left a lasting legacy.

# The Sum of This Ford's Parts: A Very Strange Car

## Alan Slatin, fifty-eight, general manager of a private country club from Lincolnshire, IL

**MY GRANDFATHER, ANDREW SLATINSKY**, worked in mechanical trades. When he retired in the late 1960s, he decided to create a hand-built vehicle that would be unlike anything else on the road, out of his home in Mattawan, Michigan.

The project began with a 1970 English-built Ford Cortina that had been damaged while being imported by ship to America. My father, Bill Slatin, worked for Ford, and was able to buy this Cortina for $1.

My grandfather drew out what he wanted, and with my father's help, he went to work. The job took three years. The four-cylinder engine and automatic transmission are original to the Cortina, and from there, he sourced parts from all over, notably from scrapyards in Kalamazoo, Michigan.

He wanted the front wheels to be outside the vehicle, with fenders that moved independently, like on a motorcycle. So the fenders and some of the front suspension come from Harley-Davidson motorcycles. At the time, a local bowling alley was getting torn down, so he procured bowling alley flooring to build a pickup bed.

He crafted door handles out of brass water-faucet parts. Much of the front end is Ford Model A from the 1920s, while the rear bumper is from a Ford Econoline van from the 1970s. He built a folding convertible top based on the design of a collapsible aluminum beach chair, and side-view mirrors are vanity mirrors with the handles machined off.

In my grandfather's community, the vehicle was a big deal. I have an old article about it from the *Kalamazoo Gazette*, circa October 1975. When Grandpa died, in 1984, the vehicle went to my brother Michael, who was instrumental in keeping it in the family. He kept it safe in storage for years.

In 2003, my dad got it running again so we could take it to Ford Motor Co.'s one-hundredth-anniversary car show in Dearborn, Michigan. Then it went into storage until 2013, when my wife Nancy and I decided to get it going. She is fond of it. It reminds her of the famous car from the movie *Chitty Chitty Bang Bang*. We use it to go to the farmers' market and things like that. It's street legal and feels very safe under 50 mph.

My father helped Grandpa build this car, and for the photos you see here, we got together again to fix it up. It needed work, and at eighty-five, my father is still a master with a wrench. The old runabout brings us together—just what I think my grandfather wanted.

*Photography by Lyndon French*

**Alan Slatin with his father, Bill, and the car their grandfather built back in the 1960s.**
**This car is made out of everything from vanity mirrors to fenders from Harley-Davidson motorcycles.**

## SPECS

Alan Slatin's Homemade Pickup

Engine: 1.5 L, inline 4-cylinder

Top Speed: 50 mph

Tires: Laramie

**SPECS**

Jean Clyde Mason's 1937 MG SA

Engine: 2 L, inline 6-cylinder

Top Speed: About 70 mph

Tires: Lester Classic

**The 1937 MG SA, a luxurious British vehicle with white-wall tires, wire-spoked wheels, and a steering wheel on the right side.**

# A Vintage 1937 MG SA That Still Turns Heads in Hollywood

### Jean Clyde Mason, eighty-four, an artist and designer from Los Angeles, CA

**MY LATE HUSBAND SPENCER** and I always loved cars. Soon after we married in 1955, we were on a game show called *You Bet Your Life*, and Groucho Marx asked the questions. We won some money and bought our first car: a three-wheeled Morgan. Soon after, we bought a used Jaguar and while I loved the look of it, I always joked that it was like being in love with an actor. It never worked. Around 1960 we were watching the 1940 film *Rebecca*, starring Laurence Olivier, when we saw this British car move across the screen. It was a 1937 MG SA. We both thought:

That is a beautiful car. Soon after, my husband saw an ad for one for sale in England. The British pound was weak at the time, so he bought the car.

The car came by boat and my husband picked it up at the dock. He drove home and said, "Come down and see your new car." I was blown away. I was working as an advertising artist and I had graduated UCLA with a design degree. To me, this was the epitome of fine design. My husband put big white-wall tires on it and I thought, this is the most glamorous car I had ever seen.

Jean Clyde Mason with her 1937 MG SA, photographed at her home in the Hollywoodland neighborhood of Los Angeles. Her husband bought this car for her, over fifty years ago.

The car ran beautifully, and I started driving it from our home in the Hollywoodland neighborhood [A.J.: near the Hollywood sign, which originally read Hollywoodland] to my advertising job downtown. We had owned English cars, so it did not bother me that the steering wheel was on the right-hand side. One of the things I loved about the MG was how it looked in our neighborhood. Many of the original homes in Hollywoodland were built before World War II, so the car fit right in.

All these years later, I still live in the same house and still drive this car. On Sundays I will drive to the top of the hill near my home and enjoy the view. Then I will drive to the Tam O'Shanter, which is a stylish English restaurant founded in 1922. They let me park in front so people can see the car.

I have had a magical life and this car has been a wonderful part of it.

**Around 1960 we were watching the 1940 film *Rebecca*, starring Laurence Olivier, when we saw this British car move across the screen.**

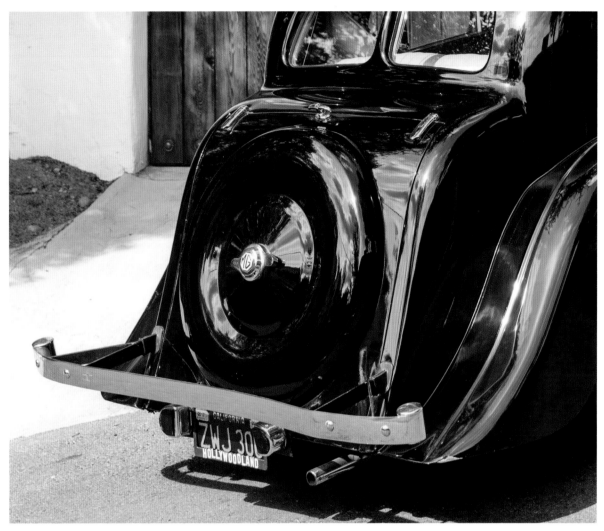

More details of the 1937 MG SA—its door handle with MG logo, the rear fender and spare tire, and gauges on the instrument panel. The old car is still driven regularly.

# The Harmon Splinter—
# A Sports Car Whittled Out of Wood
### Joe Harmon, thirty-five, an industrial designer from Mooresville, NC

**I'VE WANTED TO DESIGN** and build my own car since I was a kid. I was studying industrial design in graduate school, and I realized this was the time to do it. I wanted to take building materials—things like wood and glue—and do something with it no one else has.

I started by drawing the car on paper, in 2006, and by 2007, I began physically producing it in a shop behind my house. I had a mentor named Joe Hunt, a friend of my dad's, and my professors helped me, too. My dad gave me some money to eat, so I didn't have to focus on anything but that car. I'd wake up, work sixteen to eighteen hours, go to sleep, then do it again. Along the way I was able to pick up sponsorships—wood companies, glue companies, tool companies.

It took about twenty thousand hours to complete the car, over many years. During that time, I graduated, got a full-time job, and got married. I finished the car last fall, nearly a decade after I started, and I took it to the Essen Motor Show in Germany, to show it for the first time. It's called the Harmon

Splinter, "the world's only wooden supercar," as I call it.

The structure is made primary out of maple, ash, birch, and hickory, all woods found in North America. I wanted the body (the parts you can see) to have a certain look, so I used cherry, walnut, and oak. For these body panels, I used two large looms and wove the wood into a kind of cloth. That took a lot of work. I'll be honest—I never want to do that again. The wheels have floating spokes carved out of walnut and ash.

Many of the mechanical parts started out as Corvette components, but most have been customized. The engine is a modified LS7, the motor used in the last generation of the Corvette Z06.

Thus far, I've only driven the car about fifteen miles per hour. It has a title, but no license plate or inspection sticker. It's super low to the ground, and it's very comfortable. You can feel that it has tremendous torque and power.

It will always be a one-off. If it were to get damaged or wrecked, that'll be that.

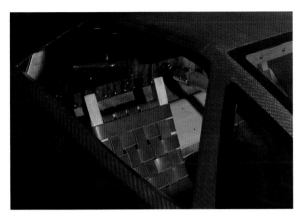

Joe Harmon built this car himself out of wood over the course of many years.
He calls it the Harmon Splinter, "the world's only wooden supercar."

It took about 20,000 hours to complete the car, over many years. During that time, I graduated, got a full-time job, and got married.

# These Aren't Your Average Muscle Cars

**Kevin Rogers, a retired machinist and stock market dabbler from Richmond, IL, and his 1970 Olds 442 and 1969 Ford Torino Talladega**

WHEN PEOPLE THINK OF MUSCLE CARS, they think Camaro, Mustang, Dodge Charger. I like different cars—cars that stand out in a crowd.

My 1970 Oldsmobile 442 was known in its day as "the banker's muscle car" because it was a little more luxurious than others. The one pictured here was owned by a buddy when I was in high school and after, so I rode around in it all the time—to and from school, Friday and Saturday nights. Some of my best memories of youth involve this car.

In the late 1980s, my buddy parked it because the maintenance and gas got too expensive. It sat for nearly twenty-five years before he let me buy it. By then it was in sorry shape, and I did an eighteen-month frame-off restoration, down to every nut and bolt.

In 2014, I took the Oldsmobile back to the old neighborhood, to the house where my buddy's mom still lives. His whole family showed up. I flipped him the keys and told him that he had "visitation rights." To this day, he's the only one but me who gets to drive this car.

My other muscle car is a 1969 Ford Torino Talladega. This is a car that I have always wanted. But it is so rare, I had never even seen one until January 2017, when I discovered the one you see here in a car dealership in Tinley Park, Illinois. It was one of those had-to-have things.

The model was originally created to race in Nascar. Ford and its racing team, Holman Moody, built an aerodynamic version of the Torino and named it Talladega after the famous Alabama superspeedway.

Ford had to build five hundred customer cars to qualify the model as a "stock car" in Nascar. About 750 were made. Mine is one of those. In racing trim, the car won the Nascar title in 1969. The people who know what my car is are floored when they see it. They cannot believe their eyes. Under the hood is the original 428 Cobra Jet engine.

These two cars represent the end of the original muscle-car era, before federal regulations cracked down on high-horsepower cars. If people knew back then how much these cars would be worth now, they would have taken better care of them.

## The people who know what my car is are floored when they see it. They cannot believe their eyes.

**SPECS**

| 1969 Ford Torino Talladega |
| --- |
| Engine: 428 cu in, V-8 |
| Top Speed: About 130 mph |
| Tires: BF Goodrich |

*Photography by Clayton Hauck*

Kevin Rogers with his two muscle cars, a 1970 Oldsmobile 442 and a 1969 Ford Torino Talladega.
The latter is a customer version of a car originally built to race in Nascar.

## SPECS

1970 Oldsmobile 442

Engine: 455 cu in, V-8

Top Speed: "Unknown because I buried the speedometer to its max 120 mph," says Rogers.

Tires: BF Goodrich

# Herbie the Love Bug Rides Yet Again

### Lynn Anderson, a vintage clothing collector from Clinton Township, MI

**I HANG OUT WITH** a bunch of guys who have movie and TV tribute cars, and we call ourselves the Motor City Reel Rides, since we live in the Detroit area. One guy has a General Lee from *The Dukes of Hazzard*, another a *Dumb & Dumber* van, another an Ecto-1 from *Ghostbusters*. I have a Herbie from *The Love Bug*.

Disney made six *Herbie the Love Bug* movies, starting with the first one in 1968, and ending with the Lindsay Lohan version, *Herbie Fully Loaded*, in 2005.

Ever since I saw the first movie as a little girl, I fell in love with Herbie. Five years ago, my husband was looking on Craigslist and he found one for sale just two hours from our house, in southern Michigan. So we drove down. There he was in a barn, covered in dust and cat paw prints. He'd been sitting there for five years. The owner had outfitted this 1965 Volkswagen Beetle as a Herbie for his wife, but she didn't drive it.

We towed him home and gave him new tires, wheels, running boards, and bumpers. He became my daily drive, at least when the weather is nice.

I'm not alone. There are hundreds of Herbies around the country (most are registered at a fan site called LoveBugFans.com). People sometimes ask: "What a cute car! What's its name?" I think: What, have you been living under a rock? When kids ask me about Herbie, I say: "Do you like the movie *Cars*, with Lightning McQueen?" They always say yes. So I say: "Herbie the Love Bug is like the Lightning McQueen of my generation."

I contacted Volkswagen and was able to get information about the car. It was born on February 27, 1965, and imported in March that year to the port of New Orleans. When I was growing up, my family was living in New Orleans in 1965. I feel like this car has been searching for me all this time.

It is over fifty years old, and requires some love and care. When I drive him, I'm not going fast—but I'm going in style.

## I'm not alone. There are hundreds of Herbies around the country (most are registered at a fan site called LoveBugFans.com).

Lynn Anderson's Herbie the Love Bug. As you might have guessed, Ms. Anderson is a big fan
of the Herbie movies, of which Disney made six.

# Radio-Control Cars: How the Pros Race

**Adam Drake, a five-time national radio-control car racing champion from Fontana, CA, and his 2006 Custom Lincoln Mark LT pickup**

LOTS OF PEOPLE HAVE played with radio-control cars, but few realize there are national- and world-level racing competitions and that there are professionals who make a living racing. I've competed in the U.S., England, Thailand, Sweden, Australia, and Italy. My wife, Ronda, is probably the best female racer in the world.

For my daily driver, I wanted something useful for my work that also celebrates my love of wheels. The best man at my wedding, Brett Oakes, is a custom-car designer who's designed vehicles for SEMA in Las Vegas—the world's largest automotive aftermarket trade show. In 2006, he offered to build me a vehicle. We started with a stock 2006 Lincoln Mark LT pickup and talked over what I'd want (nothing too flashy). I didn't see the finished truck until it was on display at SEMA in Vegas.

The paint job is off-white with a thin silver pinstripe. My racing logo is painted in pearl into the body, so you can see it only if you're looking from a certain angle. Inside are two TVs, and the stereo can practically shatter the windows. In the truck bed are four subwoofers lit up with blue LED lights, visible through plexiglass windows.

It's all about clean design and technology. The only thing missing? You can't drive it by radio-control.

## The paint job is off-white with a thin silver pinstripe. My racing logo is painted in pearl into the body . . .

**National radio-control car racing champion Adam Drake, and his wife, Ronda, whom he describes as "probably the best female racer in the world." LEFT  Their custom 2006 Lincoln pickup.**

# From World War II to Today: A Veteran and His Restored 1942 Willys Jeep

### Don Foran, ninety-one, a retired civil engineer and World War II veteran from Amarillo, TX

IN 1944, I WAS A SOLDIER assigned to the 687th Field Artillery Battalion. The Army needed Jeep drivers, so I volunteered. The Jeep was first built for World War II. It had four-wheel drive and made our Army mobile in a way it had not been before. As the saying went at the time, "It's as faithful as a dog, as strong as a mule and as agile as a goat." Willys built 362,894 Jeeps. Ford built them also, but Willys built the most.

During the collapse of Nazi Germany and after, I drove Jeeps through the country, at times behind enemy lines on scouting missions. The farm villages had no towns left. They were utterly destroyed by bombing from the air, and the cities were even more destroyed. I saw the Dachau prison camp.

In December 1945, after the war was over, I drove a Jeep to deliver documents regarding the Nazi war crimes trials

**SPECS**

| | |
|---|---|
| Don Foran's 1942 Willys Jeep | |
| Engine: 134 cu in, inline 4-cylinder | |
| Top Speed: N/A | |
| Tires: N/A | |

for many miles to Munich. The Jeep was an open vehicle and my windshield had been destroyed. It was about zero degrees, and I got lost because there were no signs. But I eventually found where I was going.

In 1992, I retired and I needed something to keep me occupied. My nephew Joe Foran spotted a 1942 Willys Jeep for sale in Gladewater, Texas. I contacted the owner and negotiated a price of $1,100. In my shop in Amarillo, I took that Jeep apart and put it back together over the course of about a year and a half. The Army was very good at making training manuals so soldiers were able to fix these Jeeps. I used a training manual to learn how each part of the Jeep worked. I also had it repainted Army green.

I drove this Jeep in local parades in Texas for years. If anyone wanted to go for a ride, I was happy to take him. I am a member of the VFW Post 430 in Canyon, Texas. Recently I signed the title over to the VFW. I have begun to give away my possessions because I am ninety-one and I realize I am not long for this world. But I still go and see the Jeep. It sure brings back memories.

# In 1944, I was a soldier assigned to the 687th Field Artillery Battalion. The Army needed Jeep drivers, so I volunteered.

Don Foran and his Willys Jeep. During World War II, Mr. Foran drove Jeeps all over Germany. Willys built 362,894 Jeeps during the war, but few still exist. Mr. Foran's is still running.

### Rainey's Reign
**Stats on Wayne Rainey, world champion motorcycle racer**

| | |
|---|---|
| 1983 | AMA Superbike Champion |
| 1987 | AMA Superbike Champion |
| 1988 | 500cc World Road Racing 3rd Place |
| 1989 | 500cc World Road Racing 2nd Place |
| 1990 | 500cc World Road Racing Champion |
| 1991 | 500cc World Road Racing Champion |
| 1992 | 500cc World Road Racing Champion |
| 1993 | 500cc World Road Racing 2nd Place |

## The kart can hit 140 mph in straights, so it's quite a weapon. At some races, we would have 30 karts from seven different countries.

*Photography by Emily Berl*

# A Superkart Puts a Paralyzed Champion Back On Wheels

### Wayne Rainey, fifty-six, a three-time Grand Prix motorcycle racing world champion and president of the MotoAmerica racing series from Carmel Valley, CA

I WAS GUNNING for a fourth consecutive MotoGP World Championship when I had my accident, in Italy in 1993. I went from being a world champion athlete to someone who needed to ask for help getting a glass out of a cupboard. Anybody who has had this kind of change in their life faces one main challenge: You wake up in the morning and you either get out of bed or you don't. I chose to get out of bed, and that's what I do every day.

The racing kart came together three years after my accident. A guy I had competed against, four-time world champion Eddie Lawson, started building the vehicle. Dan Gurney, a racing legend, built a form-fitting seat and a special hand brake, so the vehicle has a hand-operated throttle and brake like on a motorcycle. Yamaha supplied a Grand Prix motorcycle engine (about 92 horsepower), and Dunlop supplied tires.

The first time I got in the kart on a racetrack, I thought I would be as slow as a toad. My father helped me Velcro my legs down. There were fire extinguishers reachable by hand, because if there was a fire, I would not be able to get out of the kart quickly. When I started motoring, I forgot about my challenges, because I was focused on getting the best out of myself and my equipment, as I had done so many times before.

The next thing I knew, I was competing again professionally, against some of the fastest superkarters in the world, with my late father, Sandy Rainey, as my crew chief. The kart can hit 140 miles per hour in straights, so it's quite a weapon. At some races, we would have thirty karts from seven different countries. Outside of the kart, I was paralyzed, but inside, I was a racing driver, and the only limitation I had was the guy I was trying to beat.

It's been three years now since I've raced, because I'm focused on other challenges. But competitively, the kart gave me my life back. I could do things as I did before. I would just do them a little differently.

**Wayne Rainey, president of the MotoAmerica series and a three-time motorcycle racing world champion, with his racing kart. The vehicle got Mr. Rainey back on track after a horrific motorcycle crash in 1993.**

| SPECS | Wayne Rainey's Superkart |
|---|---|
| | Engine: TZ 250 cc, V-2 |
| | Top Speed: 145-plus mph |
| | Tires: Dunlop |

# How a Joker Revived a Batmobile

## Jeff Dunham, fifty-two, a comedian/ventriloquist from Los Angeles, CA, and Las Vegas, NV

**I STARTED COLLECTING** cars when my career took off. I love vehicles that get an emotional response from people. Like my Amphicar. It was an amphibious car built in the 1960s, slow and clumsy. Is it a horrible car? A horrible boat? It's both. And a 1963 Ferret Scout Car, which is a street legal tank. It's everything that a tank is, only with wheels and no live explosives.

People see these things and they're like, that's the greatest thing ever! At the same time, they're thinking, that's the most horrible thing I've ever seen.

## SPECS

Jeff Dunham's Batmobile

Engine: Corvette 7.0 L, V-8

Top Speed: "Batman abides by the traffic laws," says Dunham.

Tires: Mickey Thompson

*Photography by David Walter Banks*

# In the past few years, no matter what troubles have come along—business problems, divorce problems—I always think: Yeah . . . but I own the Batmobile!

I bought a Keaton Batmobile in 2011. It's a movie prop; it was used as the stand-in car in the filming of the 1992 Warner Bros. movie *Batman Returns*, starring Michael Keaton. I put a Corvette engine in it and reengineered things so it's drivable and safe. It has blinkers, taillights, and five cameras in it so you can see everything around you. With all the upgrades, I easily spent a half-million dollars on it.

When I go to a car show, I see all these guys with their Lamborghinis. I drive up in this plywood and fiberglass movie prop and people go nuts. It's nothing but happy.

In the past few years, no matter what troubles have come along—business problems, divorce problems—I always think: Yeah . . . but I own the Batmobile! And that makes everything okay.

Jeff Dunham and his Batmobile, originally built to be a movie prop in the Michael Keaton movie *Batman Returns*, from 1992.Mr. Dunham put a Corvette engine in and made the car roadworthy.

SPECS

Veeraindar Goli's 1950 Austin A40

Engine: 1.2 L, inline 4-cylinder

Top Speed: 71 mph

Tires: Dunlop

# A 1950 Austin A40
# Brings Back Life in India

### Veeraindar Goli, sixty-four, of Raleigh, NC, a physician and professor emeritus at Duke University School of Medicine

**I WAS BORN** not long after India gained independence from Britain. In the 1950s, India was building a lot of roads, highways, and dams, and my father was an engineer who built dams. In 1958, we lived in Delhi and he bought a 1948 Austin A40. At the time, there were many British cars in India, and Austins were popular.

I grew up with that car. In those days, if a car broke, you did not buy a new one; you fixed it. We parked the Austin outside and it survived the India-Pakistan War of 1965. At one point, my father was transferred to a town in the south. My whole family moved in the Austin. It was a three-day road trip, and at one point, the headlights went out. I remember sitting on the hood of the car holding a flashlight while my father drove through pitch-black jungle to the next town.

Later, my father taught me and my siblings to drive in this car.

We ended up selling the car in the mid-1970s and, in the late 1970s, our family began to emigrate to the U.S. We eventually settled in Raleigh, with my parents down the street from me and my family.

A few years ago, I had the idea to buy an Austin for my father's ninetieth birthday. I wanted it to be just like the car we had in India. It took three years to find this car. I searched the U.S., Australia, and India, ultimately finding this car in the U.K. I bought it for $5,000, and it arrived in April. Ironically, the cargo ship that brought it was named Delhi Highway.

The car is a 1950 model but it is virtually identical to our 1948 Austin: right-hand drive, the same color paint and interior. The car is in good shape. The seats are comfortable, the body does not have too many dents, and the original engine works fine. I believe this car is probably one of the only right-hand-drive 1950 Austin A40s in North Carolina.

My father is now ninety-three, and my mother ninety. When I presented the car to them, it was just awesome. My mother could not stop laughing because so many stories crowded her mind.

I am still restoring the Austin. Not only does it bring us happy memories, it is an important symbol of our heritage.

Veeraindar Goli, above in the center, bought this 1950 Austin as a gift for his father for his ninetieth birthday. The Goli family owned an Austin like it decades ago when they lived in India.

I am still restoring the Austin. Not only does it bring us happy memories, it is an important symbol of our heritage.

# When Your Car Is a Giant Beer Can

### George Randall, owner of retail liquor stores from Fairview Heights, IL

I LIKE WEIRD things in my garage. I have a Jack Daniel's car built out of wood with two Jack Daniel's barrels on the back and a mini Jack Daniel's barrel for a hood ornament. I have an amphibious car, and another car shaped like a P-51 Mustang fighter plane, with water guns mounted on the wings. My beer-can car is one that gets a lot of special attention. When else do you see a beer can driving down the road?

The car was built in the 1990s by a distributor of Old Milwaukee as a promotional vehicle for Old Milwaukee Light. It's built on a 1967 Volkswagen Beetle chassis with a Beetle engine, and it was used in parades and things like that. It has beer-tap handles for side-view mirrors, beer-tap handles for turn signals, and the nose of the car holds a pony keg with ice. I don't know how many miles per gallon the car gets. Wouldn't it be great if it ran on beer?

I found the car on eBay about six years ago. It was in Louisiana, and I paid $2,000 for it, plus $500 for shipping.

It's not a car you want to drive twenty or thrity miles, but around town, it's a great conversation starter. It seats two comfortably, and I take it to events and serve root beer out of it. You have no idea the flak I get sometimes, living in a suburb of St. Louis, the home of Anheuser-Busch. People yell at me, "Hey that's a Milwaukee car! Why don't you have a Budweiser car?! This is St. Louis!"

If you're wondering, I'm not a big beer guy. If I go out, I'll usually have a beer. I don't drink beer at home. But I do love this car. The thing is, we all take life so seriously. This car gets a smile and a laugh out of people. And that's a good thing.

## The thing is, we all take life so seriously. This car gets a smile and a laugh out of people. And that's a good thing.

*Photography by Whitney Curtis*

109,780.06 FL OZ.

Old Milwaukee.

**SPECS**

George Randall's Beer-Can Car

Engine: 1.8 L, 4-cylinder

Top speed: About 55 mph

Tires: Firestone

# The Airport Shuttle That Became a Lost Classic

### Liz Seibold, an entrepreneur from Washoe Valley, NV, and her 1939 Pontiac Woodie Station Wagon

TWO YEARS AGO, my husband, John, died. He left me with seventeen airplanes and forty-one cars. Of all the cars, the one pictured here is the one that will always be in our family. This story is not about how we found this car, but about how it found us.

In the 1970s, John and I became part owners of Grand Canyon Airlines. We were passionate about preserving the aviation history of the Grand Canyon, so we bought and restored some types of airplanes that the airline used in the 1930s. We also sought out previous owners of the company, and that's how we happened upon Walter Douglas of Tucson, Arizona.

When we visited Mr. Douglas, he must have been in his eighties. He had a hangar full of airplanes and cars, including this 1939 Pontiac that was originally used as a limousine to take people from Grand Canyon hotels to an airport there and back. We wanted to buy it, but Mr. Douglas was not interested.

From 1974 to 2007, we looked for another 1939 Pontiac woodie. We wanted to fix it up and put the Grand Canyon Airlines logo on it, but we never found the right car.

Then, in 2007, a chance happening occurred. A woman struck up a conversation with a guy in a laundromat in Reno, Nevada. She said her father (Walter Douglas) had left her this old Pontiac when he died. She wanted to sell it.

The man she was talking to was an employee of a friend of my husband's, so my husband got a phone call. Being a pilot, he jumped in his airplane the next day and flew from Arizona, where he was at the time, to Reno. When he saw the car, he knew it was the same one we had seen in 1974, because it had the Grand Canyon Airlines logo on it. However, the car had been sitting outside in the rain and snow for probably twenty years. One of the doors had fallen off.

We were flabbergasted. What are the chances of this happening?

John bought the car for $25,000 and had it shipped to San Diego. It went through a two-year restoration. When it was done, I thought it was the most beautiful car I had ever seen.

It was meant to be. Now, I am the owner of the woodie of my dreams.

## The car had been sitting outside in the rain and snow for probably twenty years. One of the doors had fallen off.

Liz Seibold's 1939 Pontiac Woodie

Engine: 223 cu in, inline 6-cylinder

Top Speed: N/A

Tires: Firestone

Liz Seibold and her restored 1939 Pontiac Woodie. This car was once used to shuttle travelers from Grand Canyon hotels to an airport where they flew on Grand Canyon Airlines.

# A 1952 Seagrave Firetruck: Ride of a Lifetime

### Justin Aldi, forty, a private-equity fund manager from Carmel Valley, CA

**LIKE EVERY KID** in the 1970s, I collected Tonka trucks. Unlike most, however, my passion for trucks carried into my adulthood. So I started acquiring real trucks.

My first was a 1952 Seagrave firetruck. The cost for old firetrucks is negligible; they're almost free. And they often come with meticulous documentation. This truck was purchased new by the town of Mason City, Iowa. The town built a new firehouse for this truck, and held a parade when the truck arrived. I have pictures of all of it, plus photos of the truck fighting fires and notes on every oil and tire change.

# My first was a 1952 Seagrave firetruck (pictured). The cost for old firetrucks is negligible; they're almost free. And they often come with meticulous documentation.

Later, I bought a 1959 firetruck from Mesa, Arizona, a 1927 Texaco gas truck, a 1947 Ford farm truck, and a 1952 woodie school bus that serviced the Riverdale Country School, in the Bronx. All of it is drivable, and once a week, a neighbor who's a retired firefighter comes over and helps fix anything that needs fixing.

I even named my son after a truck—Mack. (Years ago, I dragged my six-month pregnant wife to a car show in Pennsylvania, and we toured the Mack Truck factory. While walking through, I said, "Hey, there's a name for our son!")

All our trucks are unique, but they share something in common: They're powerful, and they're made in America.

# Love for Lamborghinis Brought This 1987 Jalpa Back to Life

### Derek McCallister, thirty-two, a data center technician from Redmond, OR

WHEN I WAS in high school, I became enthralled with Lamborghinis. I swore that someday I would buy one and restore it. I zeroed in on a model called Jalpa [A.J.: pronounced YAL-pa, and named for a breed of fighting bull]. This was the last V-8-powered car that Lamborghini has sold to date, and one of the last new models launched before Lamborghini was sold to Chrysler in 1987. [A.J.: The company has since come out with a new V-8 model—the Urus, the first Lamborghini SUV.]

Four and a half years ago, I found a Jalpa in New York. It was a haggard mess and needed a complete rebuild. Because it is a rare car—only 410 were made—it was not cheap. [A.J.: New in 1987, the car sold for about $65,000.] When people saw it, they said I was crazy. They said, "There's no way you can restore that car!" I thought, well, yes I can. Watch me.

It was exactly the kind of challenge that made Ferruccio Lamborghini start making cars in the first place. In the 1960s, Lamborghini was a tractor manufacturer outside Bologna, Italy. As the story goes, he bought a Ferrari that he was not happy with. When he complained, Enzo Ferrari, who lived not far away, told him to stick to tractors. So Ferruccio set out to make a better car than Ferrari could. People said, "Hey, you can't do that." Ferruccio said, "Yes I can. And I am going to love it."

I spent four years rebuilding my Jalpa in my single-car garage. The motor needed new pistons and new valves. I bored out the cylinders (to slightly over 3.5 liters) and converted the motor to electronic fuel injection. I interviewed seven machinists before I found one who could repair the cylinder heads. I took apart the interior entirely, cleaned everything, and redid the wiring. I finished the job in August.

Now it's just intoxicating. There are days when I feel like crap and I will get in that car, drive it down the street, and listen to the engine, and I feel some of the greatest happiness I have ever known.

People ask how fast it goes. I finished it just before winter hit, so I have not had the chance to stretch its legs. I am planning to get it out on Portland International Raceway and see what it can do.

> There are days when I feel like crap and I will get in that car . . . and I feel some of the greatest happiness I have ever known.

*Photography by Leah Nash*

**Derek McCallister and his Lamborghini Jalpa. Mr. McCallister restored this car himself in his single-car garage. People told him he was nuts. It was too big of a job. Look at him now.**

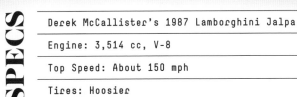

**SPECS**

Derek McCallister's 1987 Lamborghini Jalpa

Engine: 3,514 cc, V-8

Top Speed: About 150 mph

Tires: Hoosier

# The Sneaky Horsepower of a 1948 "Derelict"

**Tim Vest, fifty-two, a JetBlue pilot and co-owner of a Ford dealership from Livermore, CA**

**THE COOLEST THING** about the Derelict is the way it makes people smile. Old people love it because they remember cars from 1948. Young people love it because it reminds them of the movie *Cars*. Hot-rodders love it because they quickly figure out what it is—something completely different from what it appears.

Derelicts are the dream children of a custom-car builder from Los Angeles named Jonathan Ward, whose company is called Icon. From the outside, the Derelict looks like an old machine with tons of character. Underneath, it is fully modern—a stealth high-performance vehicle. Ward has made

fewer than a dozen, and each is unique.

I met Ward when I hired him to work on a different project. He had built a Derelict station wagon for himself, and I loved the idea. He found a 1948 Buick Super 8 on Craigslist, and in 2013, I bought it and had it shipped to his shop. The Buick had not been driven since 1959, and you could see all the patina, the dents and rust, even a stain on the fender where someone had left a rag sitting for decades.

The build took two years. Ward took the body off and scanned it, then had a custom frame made by Art Morrison, a chassis builder. The brakes are Wilwood, the steering is

SPECS

Tim Vest's Buick Derelict

Engine: 6.2 L, supercharged V-8

Top Speed: About 160 mph

Tires: Goodyear

state-of-the-art, and we got high-performance tires. The motor was an important decision. I chose an LS9 Corvette engine, tuned so it puts out over 650 horsepower. We also had a new stereo tucked into the dash under the old one. Back-up camera, navigation, air-conditioning, power seats, and windows—everything you'd find in a new car.

The wheels are the only modern pieces visible to the eye, so we downplayed them—custom wheels and hubcaps painted so the color blends in with the vehicle's rust.

While the Derelict is not cheap (mine cost well into the six figures), it drives like a new BMW 7 Series. I can motor down Highway 17 into Santa Cruz with two fingers on the wheel. When I shoot past a car on those windy curves, I love to see the expression on the driver's face. He's thinking: What the hell is that?

It's a Buick Derelict—one of a kind.

**From the outside, the Derelict looks like an old machine with tons of character. Underneath, it is fully modern—a stealth high-performance vehicle.**

*Photography by Angela DeCenzo*

## Beat-Up, Bad-Ass  A shortlist of other Icon Derelicts, on the road today

1. 1966 Ford Bronco Roadster Derelict with a Ford Mustang GT V-8

2. 1949 GMC Derelict pickup with a 430 hp V-8

3. 1946 Oldsmobile Derelict with a 600 hp V-8

4. 1961 Volkswagen split-window bus Derelict with a modern water-cooled four-cylinder

5. The original Derelict: a 1952 DeSoto station wagon with a 6. 1 L Hemi fuel-injected V-8

# A 1967 Chevrolet Camaro—
# Living the High School Dream

## Stanley Morrical, fifty-eight, an employee-benefits broker in San Francisco, CA

**MY DAD BOUGHT** the Camaro you see here in 1977. I had just gotten my driver's license, and I would stand in our garage in Fort Wayne, Indiana, drooling. This was a dream car for a long-haired kid in the late 1970s, but my father was not enthusiastic about me driving it. He thought I would get in trouble. He was probably right. I went off to college and, in 1982, my father died of a heart attack. He was only forty-five.

For thirteen years, the Camaro sat in my mother's garage, but I never forgot about it. The model year 1967 was the very first year of the Camaro, which Chevrolet launched to battle Ford's Mustang. This specific Camaro came with the Super Sport package—high performance.

In the mid-1990s, my business in San Francisco was doing well, and I finally had some money. Through my work I met a guy named Jack Nilson. He was a drag racer and he owned a garage near the Sears Point racetrack in Sonoma [A.J.: now known as Sonoma Raceway].

He convinced me to take my dad's old Camaro to his shop. Over ten years, together, we built out the Camaro as I would have done if I had had money back when I was a teenager.

The process was like redoing an old house. You do one thing and then realize that there are all these other things you have to do. For example, when we reupholstered the back seats, we realized we needed new carpeting and a new headliner [A.J.: the fabric on the underside of the roof].

Purists will roll their eyes at some of the stuff we did, but I wanted to build the car I wanted. We put in more comfortable front seats and air-conditioning. The original engine was a 350 V-8, and we replaced it with a new 350 that puts out more horsepower—385—plus disc brakes to handle that extra power.

My father probably spent less than $1,000 on this car. I spent more than that on one wheel. If he knew how much I spent on it, he would die of a heart attack a second time. But for me, this Camaro is more than a vehicle; it's my dream car and a tribute to my memory of him.

**SPECS**

Stanley Morrical's 1967 Chevrolet Camaro SS

Engine: 350 cu in, V-8

Top Speed: About 140 mph

Tires: BF Goodrich

# My father probably spent less than $1,000 on this car. I spent more than that on one wheel.

## All-American Muscle
### Stanley Morrical's dream garage

1.  1967 Chevrolet Camaro

2.  1970 Plymouth Road Runner Superbird

3.  1970 Ford Boss Mustang

4.  1967 Chevrolet Chevelle

5.  1970 Chevrolet Chevelle

6.  1964 Chevrolet Corvette

7.  1961 Cadillac Convertible

8.  1967 Lincoln Convertible (with suicide doors)

9.  1957 Porsche 356 Speedster Convertible

10. 1966 Pontiac GTO

**Stanley Morrical and his 1967 Chevrolet Camaro. The model year 1967 was the first for the Camaro, built to take on Ford's Mustang. It has since become an automotive icon.**

# The 1950 Studebaker Champion Design Nerds Go Gaga Over

## Tracey Smith, an executive vice president at the automotive company Carroll Shelby International, from San Pedro, CA

**I USED TO HAVE** a bad habit of staying up late and playing around on eBay. One night in 2006, I put in a bid for a Studebaker. It was midnight, and my bid was low ($3,000), so I did not think I would win. I woke up the next morning and the car was mine. I was like, "Oh crap, now what?"

When the car showed up at my house on a transporter, it was a disaster. It had been sitting on this nice old man's lawn in Oregon for years. It took months to restore the car so it could become, for a time, my daily driver.

The Champion "bullet nose" (named for the chrome bullet on the front) has a unique place in auto history. It was only built for two model years, and it was designed by the firm of

SPECS

Tracey Smith's 1950 Studebaker Champion

Engine: 170 cu in, inline 6-cylinder

Top Speed: About 80 mph

Tires: B.F. Goodrich

Raymond Loewy. Loewy is often called the father of industrial design. He is known for the logos of Exxon, Shell, and Lucky Strike cigarettes. He designed the paint job on John F. Kennedy's Air Force One, and even helped design the interior of America's first space station.

For me, his most enduring design remains the bullet nose. The car was built soon after World War II. It was a new age of aviation, and the nose was inspired by aircraft. The joke about these strangely designed Studebakers has always been that you cannot tell if the car is coming or going, because, from the profile, you can't tell which side is the front or back. You could slap the headlights on either end.

One year, just before Christmas, my car went missing from the garage where I work. My boss—the late Carroll Shelby, an automotive icon—took the car, pulled out the engine, and had it restored, as a gift. It was such a sweet thing to do, and it made the car even more special.

Driving the car requires an upper-body workout. Parallel parking in L.A. is like doing Pilates. But that's part of the Champion's charm. It takes a while to get her going. But when you do, she floats down the road.

# Driving the car requires an upper-body workout. Parallel parking in L.A. is like doing Pilates. But that's part of the Champion's charm.

Tracey Smith's 1950 Studebaker Champion. The vehicle is nicknamed "bullet nose" for the
strange bullet-like chrome on the front end. The styling was inspired by the new age of 1950s aviation.

# One Laker's Antidote for L.A. Traffic: His 2017 Tesla Model X 100D

### Corey Brewer, thirty-one, a six-foot-nine forward with the Los Angeles Lakers in his eleventh NBA season

I LIVE IN THE VALLEY, and my team practices in El Segundo. I have played for a lot of basketball teams and lived in a lot of cities, and I will tell you, there is no traffic like the traffic in L.A. It can take forty-five minutes to go four miles on I-405. I decided to buy a Tesla because it is an electric car, so I could go in the HOV lane when I am by myself, and because it has an autopilot function, so the car is supposed to basically drive itself.

The process of buying the car was unlike anything I have experienced. You go online and pick out what you want—the color, the color of the rims, how many seats you want. [A.J.: The car can come with five, six, or seven.] A few weeks later, the car is ready. I spent about $115,000, and I got the car home in September. The rear doors are falcon-wing doors. I put my son Sebastian's car seat in the back and he freaked out when he saw these doors open. He thought the car was the Batmobile.

There is no gas tank. Each night, I plug the car into

SPECS

| Corey Brewer's 2017 Tesla Model X |
| --- |
| Engine: 100 kWh battery |
| Top Speed: About 155 mph |
| Tires: N/A |

*Photography by Emily Berl*

a wall outlet. At the practice facility, there is a charging station that works much faster. [A.J.: Tesla claims a range of 295 miles when fully charged.]

The first time I turned on the autopilot, I was thinking, is this really going to work? It does! The car has cameras and radar so it will stay in its lane automatically. If the car in front slows down or stops, my car does the same. You have to pay attention, but you can enjoy the ride. Also, the Model X is really comfortable for tall people.

My first car was a 1994 Eagle Talon. I was sixteen years old, working at a Hardee's fast-food place in Tennessee making, I think, $5.15 an hour. I saved up and bought the car for $1,000. Every now and then, I pass a Carl's Jr. in my Tesla. In California, Hardee's is called Carl's Jr. I'll cruise by—the car doing most of the driving by itself—and I think, man, I have come a long way.

# One Little Red Corvette Leads to Another

## Kim Burroughs, a dentist from Gambrills, MD, and her 1962 Chevrolet Corvette

**WHEN I WAS LITTLE,** my sister and I both had Barbie dolls and Barbie Corvettes, which were toy cars that Barbie "drove." Mine was purple, my sister's was silver, and we played with them all the time.

Jump forward to 1997. My father John Burroughs bought a 1959 Corvette. I helped him push the car off the trailer when it was delivered to his house in Sunderland, Maryland. I was starting dental school in the Baltimore area, so I was not around to help him restore it. He promised that this car would be mine someday, but I guess I got impatient.

In 2015, my boyfriend Scott Chalk—who restores cars professionally—told me about a friend who had a 1962 Corvette that he had gotten in the 1970s. He had taken it apart intending to restore it but that never happened, and now he wanted to sell it. We went and saw the car; it had been painted red and all the parts were in boxes.

The year 1962 was the last of the first-generation Corvette, and the best in my opinion because the car came with a bigger 327 V-8 engine. In June 2015, I paid $30,000 for mine. My boyfriend and I loaded it in a trailer and brought it home. We created lists of all the parts we had and all the parts we needed. I went to swap meets and Corvette shows to find parts. We spent some sixty hours underneath the car scraping off undercoating, which had probably been put on by a dealership when the car was originally purchased.

The underside of the trunk lid was still the original paint color, so a paint specialist used that to mix the right shade, which was called Honduras Maroon.

Along the way, we realized that our restoration was going to be really nice, so we decided to have the car judged by the National Corvette Restorers Society, which looks at how close a restorer can get a car to what it was the day it left the factory.

We finished our restoration in October 2016, which is fast for a job this big. On April 8, 2018, we took the car to be judged by the Mason Dixon chapter of the NCRS, in Havre de Grace, Maryland. The car earned a "Top Flight" award, the highest you can get.

To think, it all started with a Barbie doll.

## SPECS

| | |
|---|---|
| Kim Burroughs's 1962 Chevrolet Corvette | |
| Engine: | 327 cu in, V-8 |
| Top Speed: | About 125 mph |
| Tires: | B.F. Goodrich |

# How an 1978 AMC Pacer Became a Showstopper

### Matt Caccamo, thirty-six, a lawyer from Chicago, IL

THE PACER IS NOT your average car. You always find it on those quirky lists: Ugliest cars of all time. Nerdiest cars of all time. It's been called the Pregnant Gremlin and the Flying Fishbowl because it has so much glass. It's probably the only car ever designed with the passenger side door four inches longer than the driver's side door, so people can get in and out of the back seat easier. The car's builder, AMC, disappeared in the late 1980s, which to me only adds to this car's weird charm.

In July 2014, my girlfriend at the time, Kathryn Williams, and I went to take a look at an old Pacer a guy was selling five minutes from where she was living. I wasn't planning on buying a car, but things sort of lined up. The car was from 1978. I was born in 1979. Kathryn was born in 1980. I love stuff from the 1970s—clothes, electronics, and especially cars. But it was Kathryn who really fell for the Pacer. That sealed the deal for me.

We took it for a spin, paid $3,900, and drove off in it the next week. It was the first car we bought together, and soon after, we were engaged and married, so a drive in the Pacer now feels like it's all destiny.

The car is like a dog. Normally strangers don't approach you. But if they see you have a dog, they'll come up and talk to you like they know you. Same with the Pacer. One stranger came up to us to tell us he had an old hubcap from a 1978 Pacer. Did we want it? Another told us he'd once driven a Pacer up Mount Rainier. Ours struggles up little hills in Chicago; how this guy got one up Rainier, I have no idea.

Car guys want to talk about the engine specs. Young people just want to know what the Pacer is, because they've never seen one. Mostly, people are just surprised the owner is younger than the car. People ask: "Is that your Dad's car?" Nope, it's mine, and my wife's.

## People are just surprised the owner is younger than the car. People ask: "Is that your Dad's car?" Nope, it's mine, and my wife's.

**SPECS**

Matt Caccamo's 1978 AMC Pacer

Engine: 258 cu in, inline 6-cylinder

Top speed: 101 mph

Tires: Tiger Paw

Matt Caccamo and his wife Kathryn, with their AMC Pacer. The Pacer has been nicknamed everything from the Pregnant Gremlin to the Flying Fishbowl. The Caccamos bought theirs in 2014 for $3,900.

*Photography by Katrina Wittkamp*    **MY RIDE 93**

## I was scared the first time I drove it in the driveway. But I'm not scared anymore.

Talan Drake and his kart, which can hit about 60 mph. The young racer and his dad travel all over to compete. "I like to win," he says, "but making friends is a big part of it too."

**SPECS**

| Talan Drake's Merlin/Yamaha racing kart | |
| --- | --- |
| Engine: 100 cc | |
| Top Speed: Between 58 and 65 mph | |
| Tires: N/A | |

# Fourth-Grader Has License to Drive

**Talan Drake, ten, from Riverside, IA, and his Merlin/Yamaha racing kart**

**WHEN I WAS FIVE**, my dad took me to a go-kart race in Mount Joy, Iowa. On the way home, I said, "I want to do that!" So my dad got me a go-kart. I was scared the first time I drove it in the driveway. But I'm not scared anymore.

For five years, I've raced in Route 66, which is a regional go-kart series. On race weekends, we leave home on Thursday night or Friday morning, and we've raced in Illinois, Missouri, Florida, Indiana, North and South Carolina, Pennsylvania, Wisconsin, Minnesota, and Iowa. I miss school on those Fridays, but my teacher gives me my work to take with me.

The kart I'm racing now, I won—not at a race, but in a raffle at an end-of-the-year Route 66 banquet. It's a Merlin kart, and it runs on gasoline. You can change a sprocket [A.J.: before a race]—the higher the gear, the faster the kart can go through corners. The lower, the faster it'll go on straightaways. Top speed is about sixty miles per hour. We tow the kart in an enclosed trailer that also has wheels, gas, my helmet, and safety gear.

I came in tenth in this year's first race, and the next one is next month in Shawano, Wisconsin. I like to win, but making friends is a big part of it, too.

# A Speeding Ticket Ignited a Passion for Aston Martin Vulcan and One-77

### Joe Clark of Seattle, co-founder and chairman of Aviation Partners, the maker of aerodynamic wing tips for Boeing aircraft

WHEN I WAS SIXTEEN, my father made some money in the natural-gas business, and the first thing he did was buy a 1958 Aston Martin DB2/4 MkIII. A week later he was going out of town and he told me, "Don't you dare drive that car."

Of course, I did. I got pulled over for speeding and ended up in court. My dad was furious, but I was left with a lifelong passion for Aston Martins.

I now have five, including my father's 1958 model. The two you see pictured here are the most extreme Aston Martin customer cars ever built.

The pearl-white car is a One-77. Only seventy-seven were built, with no two exactly alike, and I took delivery of mine in 2015. My father's old Aston put out around 160 horsepower. This car has a V-12 capable of 750, with a 220 miles per hour top speed. It has a placard saying "Hand Built for Joe Clark," and we came up with a special color—Olympic white, named for the Olympic Mountains near where I live.

No other car has this exact color.

A Ferrari may be beautiful, but this car has an unmatched elegance. You can look at it from any angle and it appears perfect, like a fine diamond.

The other car, which I took delivery of last year, is called Vulcan. It is a gentleman's race car, built only for the track, and I have driven it on racetracks in the U.S. and Europe. The V-12 has three modes: 550 horsepower, 675, and 820, and the first time I drove the car, I had to do about thirty laps with a professional race-car driver before I could switch out of the first mode. The power is that extreme, and the downforce from aerodynamics is so strong, the car can carry speeds of over 170 miles per hour into turns.

I have been an aviation man all my life. This car feels more like fighter planes I have flown than an automobile.

Each of these cars cost over $2 million. I have been offered double that for them, but I bought them to drive, not to sell.

SPECS

| Joe Clark's Aston Martin One-77 |
| --- |
| Engine: 7.3 L, V-12 |
| Top Speed: 220 mph |
| Tires: Michelin |

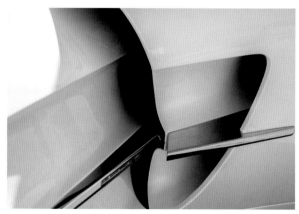

**SPECS**

| | |
|---|---|
| Joe Clark's Aston Martin Vulcan | |
| Engine: 7L, V-12 | |
| Top Speed: Over 200 mph | |
| Tires: N/A | |

Joe Clark owns several Aston Martins, including a 1958 Aston his father owned before him—
the car that inspired his love for the British carmaker. Below: His One-77 and his Vulcan.

# 1959 Edsel Corsair:
# The Clunker-Turned-Classic

## Ken Lammert, eighty-two, a retired mechanic and service station owner from Affton, MO

**THIS PAST** Saturday, crowds braved winter weather in St. Louis to watch the forty-eighth annual St. Patrick's Day Parade. In the parade, I drove my 1959 Edsel with Ms. Senior America Peggy Lee Brennan in the car. By my estimate, it had to be the five hundredth parade my Edsel has been in.

The Edsel started out as probably the most infamous car ever known. Ford launched the Edsel line in September 1957, with the biggest advertising campaign I remember ever seeing, at the time. The car was named after Henry Ford's only son, Edsel. By November 1959, Ford announced the end of Edsel production, and it was considered a huge failure.

I owned a service station and I had a contract for all the warranty work at a Lincoln-Mercury dealership, and in December 1959, I saw an Edsel sitting on the dealership lot. I liked it so much I bought it on a whim, for $2,245 plus my 1954 Ford.

When I got home, my wife gave me hell. We were expecting our third child. A convertible wasn't practical.

The car was expensive and she was furious. When my father saw the car, he said, "Why did you go and buy that piece of junk?" It felt like the talk of the town. Everyone thought I was a fool for buying an Edsel.

Over the years, the response has changed. My Edsel has proven to be a great vehicle. It has over 359,000 miles on it and it is still running. Even my father came around. I moved my family to Houston and he would come down and want to see the car.

When I drive it now, every eye on the street turns. The older generation knows what the car is, so these people get excited. Young people do not know what it is, but they love it too.

The Edsel has become a piece of Americana, which is why I drive it in so many parades. I have had numerous dignitaries in this car—mayors, congressmen, even an astronaut. I keep an American flag on the car all the time. I guess buying the Edsel back in 1959 was not such a bad idea after all.

Ken Lammert in his 1959 Edsel. When Ford produced this car in the late 1950s, it was considered a disaster and a joke. Today, Edsels are cult classics.

*Photography by Whitney Curtis*

**SPECS**

Ken Lammert's 1959 Edsel Corsair

Engine: 361 cu in, V-8

Top speed: "I've had it up to 110 mph," says Ken.

Tires: Uniroyal

# A 1969 Plymouth Barracuda Mod Top That Runs on Flower Power

### Kim Barnes, the event director for the Art in Motion Concours d'Elegance at New York's Monticello Motor Club, from Pylesville, MD

GROWING UP, I loved cars, and in 1969, I used to ride my bike two miles to a Chrysler dealership in Des Moines, Iowa, to see this new vehicle in the window. It was a yellow Plymouth Barracuda Mod Top, and it had this gorgeous floral design on the roof and seats. [A.J.: Plymouth was a division of Chrysler, defunct in 2001.]

The story was, Chrysler executives in the 1960s realized that women were buying their own cars rather than their husbands buying cars for them. More and more women were getting jobs and making choices for themselves, and Chrysler wanted a car that would appeal to them.

Company executives came up with this idea of floral roofs and seats, and partnered with another company that specialized in shower curtains and tablecloths to make patterned vinyl that did not fade in the sun. Chrysler called the car Mod Top, and advertised it as "The Car You Wear."

The Mod Top was not originally a success, so only 937 1969 Mod Top Barracudas were made. It took me about forty years to find mine. I passed on two six-cylinder Mod Tops, but then, just before Christmas in 2015, I saw one with the more powerful V-8, for sale on eBay. My husband already thought I had too many cars—I have a small collection—so I was reluctant to bring it up. In the end, I could not help myself.

The car was in Texas. I bought it sight unseen and had it transported to my house. My daily driver is a 2017 Jeep Wrangler Unlimited Sahara, and this Mod Top cost roughly the same as that car.

Six months later, I took it to the Carlisle Chrysler Nationals, in Carlisle, Pennsylvania—a huge gathering for Chrysler fans. There was one other 1969 Barracuda Mod Top at the show, and the owner had the original paperwork. When I looked at it, I could not believe my eyes.

His car had been purchased in 1969 from the same Iowa dealership that I used to go to as a kid, where I first saw a Mod Top. Chrysler made so few of these, and this one had the same yellow paint, so it had to be the exact car. It was a wonderful moment, for me and my Mod Top.

## SPECS

| | |
|---|---|
| Kim Barnes's 1969 Plymouth Barracuda Mod Top | |
| Engine: 318 cu in, V-8 | |
| Top Speed: 111 mph | |
| Tires: Uniroyal Tiger Paw | |

*Photography by Matt Roth*

**The Mod Top was not originally a success, so only 937 1969 Mod Top Barracudas were made. It took me about 40 years to find mine.**

Kim Barnes with her 1969 Plymouth Barracuda Mod Top. Chrysler built this car to appeal to women buyers, partnering with a shower curtain maker to create the floral-patterned vinyl roof.

# It's a Car! No. It's a Boat!
# No. It's a 1964 Amphicar!

### Jim Golomb, sixty-five, a retired businessman from Northfield, IL

**LIFE'S MORE INTERESTING** when you drive fun cars. The Amphicar was built in West Germany from 1961 to 1968. The pitch was, you're buying a car and a boat, as it was, in fact, both. Unfortunately, it wasn't a very good car, nor a good boat. It was called a Model 770, because it was supposed to go seven knots in water, and seventy miles per hour on road. I think it's more of a 550—five knots in water, and fifty miles per hour on road. The engine only puts out forty-three horsepower. But you can't measure the car's ability to amuse.

The Amphicar became famous because Lyndon Johnson owned one. He'd drive people around on his Texas ranch,

then head for a pond yelling, "The brakes don't work! . . . We're going under!" Then he'd roar with laughter, motoring into the pond.

I first saw an Amphicar off Chicago's Navy Pier, in Lake Michigan. In 2009, I found one for sale for $15,000 on eBay. The engine was frozen and the transmission gummed up, and there were big holes in the vehicle—nothing time and money couldn't fix.

To take in water, you have to make sure the bilge plug is in, and there's a locking mechanism that seals the doors closed. You engage the two propellers with a shifting mechanism, then you drive into the water. When you take the

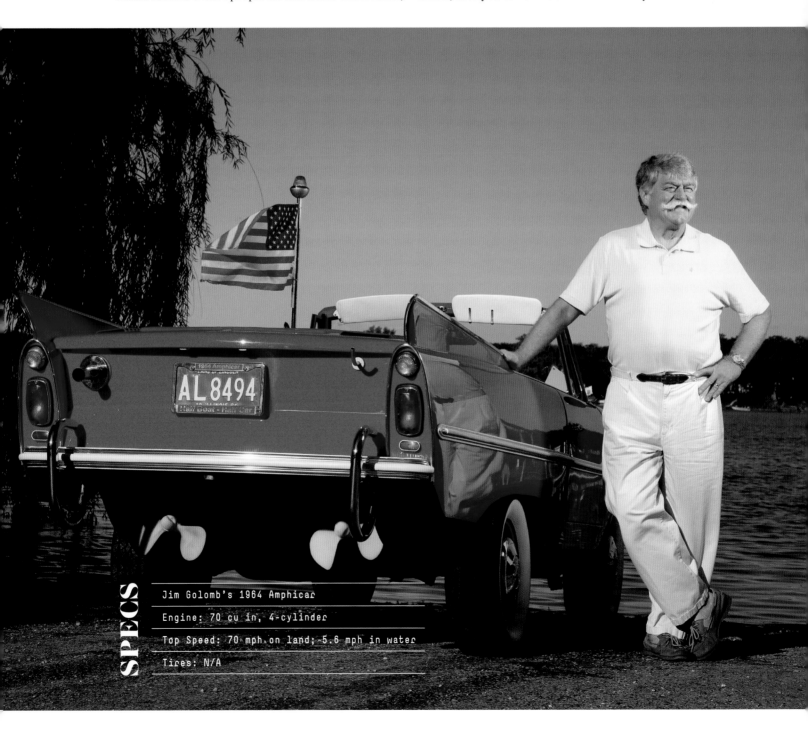

SPECS

Jim Golomb's 1964 Amphicar

Engine: 70 cu in, 4-cylinder

Top Speed: 70 mph on land; 5.6 mph in water

Tires: N/A

*Photography by Katrina Wittkamp*

car out of gear, the propellers can push while the wheels aren't turning. You steer by turning the front wheels, only the turning radius is horrible. Let's just say turning takes a while.

When you go boating, people can't believe what they're seeing. I've heard stories about the police showing up, because someone called them on their cellphone: "Oh my God! Someone drove a car in the water!"

Sometimes at car shows, kids will walk by looking at their smartphones. They don't even notice Ferraris. I say, "Hey kids, this car has propellers." They look at the Amphicar and yell, "Mom! Dad! Look at this! This is the coolest car I've ever seen!" It's an attraction, to say the least.

**Jim Golomb and his 1964 Amphicar—an amphibious vehicle he says is neither a good car, nor a good boat. "But," he says, "you can't measure the car's ability to amuse."**

# The Amphicar became famous because Lyndon Johnson owned one. He'd drive people around on his Texas ranch, then head for a pond yelling, "The brakes don't work!"

# The Million-Mile 1976 Chevrolet G10

### William Brotherton, sixty-five, an attorney from Argyle, TX

THE GUYS AT MY LOCAL car dealership were always amazed with my van, because it had so many miles on it with the original engine. Recently, the van clicked over a million miles. So they threw it a thirty-ninth birthday party. They detailed it and rolled it onto the showroom floor for a few days with a banner: "Happy 39th Birthday Ole Blue!"

I was working as a sewage-treatment plant operator in Atlanta when I first bought my 1976 Chevrolet G10 van, new for $3,600. Things like power steering and a V-8 engine were options, so to keep the price down, I got the basic van with a six-cylinder.

Over the next few years, I worked at a potato-processing plant in North Dakota, then as a railroad brakeman all over the place. I was short on funds, so I built a bed in the back of the Chevy, and my wife sewed curtains. We had a little icebox and a stove, and I slept in the van. We started having kids and we went everywhere in the van, through every one of the lower forty-eight states, across the Trans-Canada Highway, down into Mexico.

We thought nothing about throwing the kids, dogs, tents, and a playpen in there, and driving a thousand miles. There were no seat belts, but luckily we survived.

The worst thing that ever happened to the van was a flat tire. Once, I was driving home from Texarkana when the steering wheel broke. I had to finish the drive with half a steering wheel. I've changed the battery and tires innumerable times. The van has fresh paint and new front seats. But the engine and transmission are original.

I chuckle when I see the old bed in the back where I slept when I was a railroad brakeman. I have my own law practice now in Texas, and the van keeps me humble. It's a rolling memory machine.

Recently, my oldest grandson, Max, said, "Papa, when you die, can I have the van?" My oldest daughter said, "No way, I'm getting it next." It's still got many miles left in it, and it's going to stay in the family for a long time.

## We thought nothing about throwing the kids, dogs, tents, and a playpen in there, and driving a thousand miles. There were no seat belts, but luckily we survived.

*Photography by Brandon Thibodeaux*

William Brotherton bought this 1976 Chevrolet G10 van for $3,600 new. When the van hit a million miles, a Chevy dealership threw it a party. Mr. Brotherton calls it a "Rolling Memory Machine."

SPECS

William Brotherton's 1976 Chevrolet G10

Engine: 350 cu in, V-8

Top Speed: About 90 mph

Tires: BF Goodrich

# In my opinion, there are only two real independent hypercar builders today: Koenigsegg of Sweden and Pagani of Italy.

## SPECS

| | |
|---|---|
| Jeffrey Cheng's 2008 Koenigsegg CCX | |
| Engine: 4.7 L, V-8 | |
| Top Speed: 245-plus mph | |
| Tires: N/A | |

Jeffrey Cheng and his 2008 Koenigsegg CCX.
The Swedish car is capable of speeds well over 200 mph—just
the thing for a commute to work in Los Angeles.

# The Swedish 2008 Koenigsegg CCX Ferrari Owners Envy

## Jeffrey Cheng, a private-equity investor from Newport Beach, CA

YEARS AGO, THE WORD "supercar" came into vogue. A supercar is a rare, expensive performance automobile, like a Ferrari or a Lamborghini. Later, car fans started using the word "hypercar." These vehicles are even more exclusive—so rare in fact, you are not likely to ever even catch a glimpse of one. They can cost well over a million dollars, and they pack so much power, they defy the whole idea of what a car is supposed to be.

In my opinion, there are only two real independent hypercar builders today: Koenigsegg of Sweden and Pagani of Italy.

I was lucky enough to see a Koenigsegg at a gas station in 2009. I was already a Ferrari collector, and I knew of this car and its ingenious creator, Christian von Koenigsegg. I was transfixed. The vehicle looked like nothing I had ever seen.

A few years later, I got a call from a specialty car dealer in Seattle saying he had a Koenigsegg CCX for sale. Within twenty-four hours, I was at his dealership handing him a check. With a car this rare, I feared that I would never have another shot at one.

Koenigsegg was founded in Sweden in 1994 by then-twenty-year-old Christian von Koenigsegg, and to this day, only 134 cars have been completed. [AJ: This column was published on June 20, 2017.] The CCX was the first Koenigsegg imported into the U.S. The experience of driving it is hard to put into words. The engine puts out 806 horsepower. The vehicle is very lightweight and full of suspension technology, so this power is delivered in a smooth, refined manner. Top speed is over 245 mph.

At the time I bought my CCX, there was no place to service my car, so a Koenigsegg technician flew in to do the work in my garage.

Last summer I drove the CCX to Monterey Car Week, a huge gathering of enthusiasts. A mob crowded around. It was as if a spaceship had landed.

Koenigsegg is building a new car called Agera RS. As very few are slated for the U.S. I ordered one and it is scheduled to arrive in July. This new car will put well over one thousand horsepower to the pavement. I cannot wait to get behind the wheel.

**I'm a third-generation pilot. Not even
the sensation of taking off in an airplane can
compare to the sense of being carried away.**

# A Driver Fixated on Her Four Ferraris

### Julie Ibrahim, a retailer from Anderson, SC

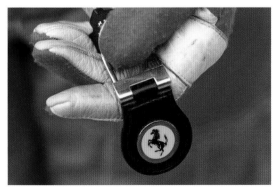

**THIS MONTH,** Ferrari owners across the country will descend on the California coast for the Pebble Beach Concours d'Elegance and the Ferrari Club of America International Meet, in Monterey. I'll be there. [A.J.: This article original ran in the *Wall Street Journal* in August 2015.]

My late husband instilled the passion for these cars in me. We bought our house because, in part, it had belonged to a Ferrari racer, and we started a Ferrari club event that I still host at the house every year. My husband passed away in 2008, and I'm fortunate enough to have four of the Ferraris he bought, including a 1971 365 GTB/4 Daytona and an F40, which celebrated the company's fortieth anniversary in 1987.

People ask me: What is it about these cars that inspires such adoration? There's a magic about them. It's about the history, the art, the racing successes and the prestige around the world. But mostly it's the experience of driving them.

All are unique, but the F40 is extra special to me, because it was the last Ferrari my husband and I bought together, and it was his crowning achievement as a collector. Every time I drive it, I think of him. I've reached about 160 miles per hour in this car on a track. I'm a third-generation pilot. Not even the sensation of taking off in an airplane can compare to the sense of being carried away.

I guess I'm just a Ferrari girl.

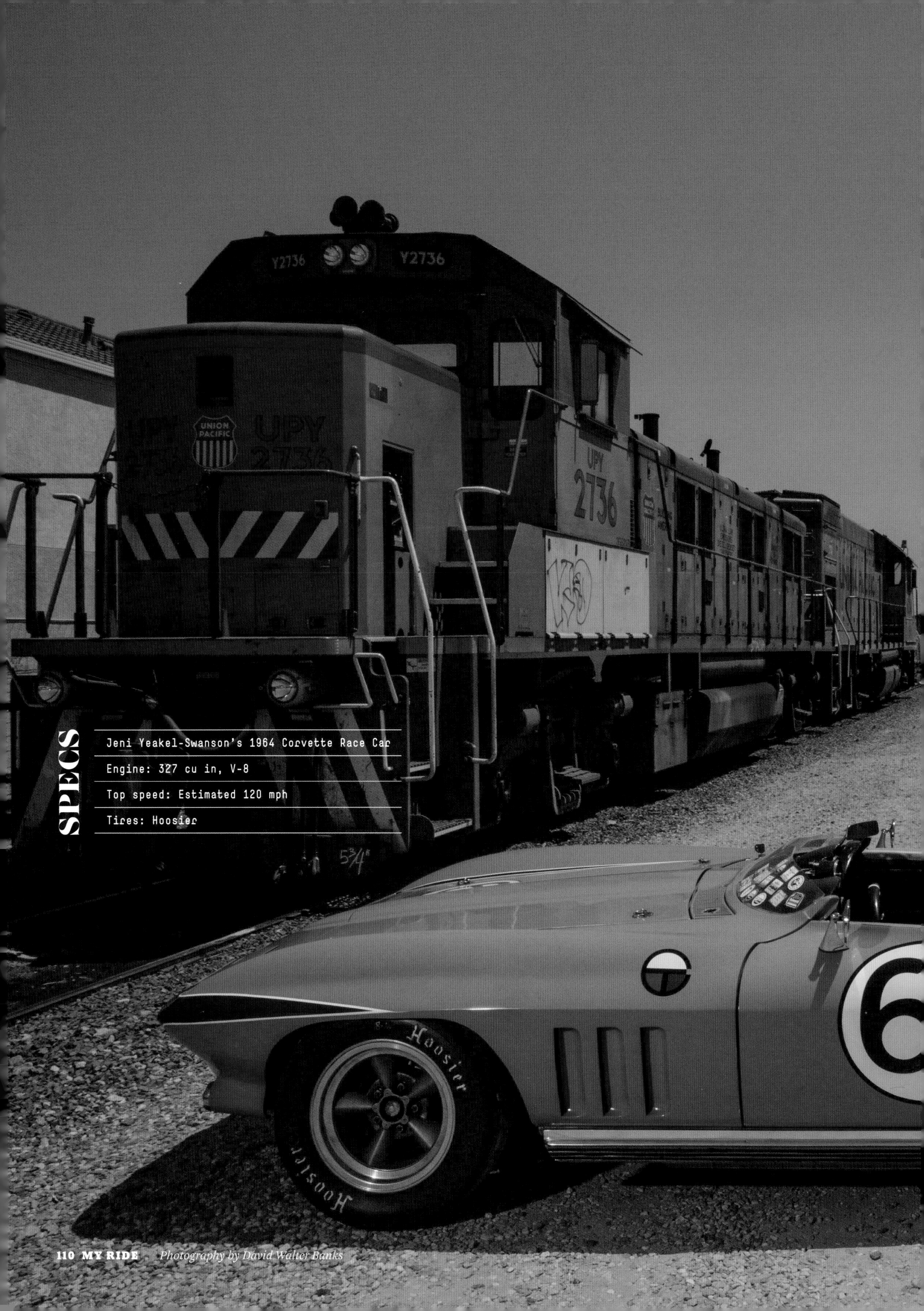

## SPECS

Jeni Yeakel-Swanson's 1964 Corvette Race Car

Engine: 327 cu in, V-8

Top speed: Estimated 120 mph

Tires: Hoosier

 *Photography by David Walter Banks*

# Don't Mess with This "Nuclear Carrot" Corvette

**Jeni Yeakel-Swanson, a real-estate lawyer in San Diego, CA, and her 1964 Chevrolet Corvette Race Car**

WHEN I WAS growing up, my dad, Fred Yeakel, raced a 1957 Corvette. I went to races with him, and when I was old enough, I told him, "Dad, I want to drive!" He said, "First you have to learn how to work on the car."

He taught me all about how that 1957 Corvette worked, and ultimately, I started driving on a racetrack. I said, "There's no horsepower in this car." He said, "You don't need horsepower to drive well. Learn to drive well, then we will add horsepower." Which is exactly what we did.

In 2007, he found the car pictured here in an ad in *Vintage Motorsport* magazine. It was painted red and the owner had it in storage outside Milwaukee. When we bought it, it came with documentation on its history. An Illinois-based driver had purchased the vehicle (it had been a theft recovery) and built it out as a race car in the 1960s. A piece of the front was missing, so he used parts he got from a junkyard.

Using old photos, my dad restored the car to what it had been in the 1960s. He was driving a Bill Thomas Cheetah race car at the time, and I like to think that he bought the Corvette for me. I have been the primary driver and my name is painted on the car next to the original sponsor from the 1960s—Tero Corvette of Rolling Meadows, Illinois.

We started going to races up and down the West Coast, from San Diego to Portland, Oregon. We trailered our cars together, had our pits side by side, and sometimes even raced against one another. Along the way, a family friend, the late Mike Scott, gave this car its nickname: Nuclear Carrot.

Last year, under my dad's supervision, I rebuilt the 327 V-8. I took it apart and put it back together with new rods, pistons, the works.

Our next race will be at Sonoma Raceway, in the spring. To get the car ready, I will drive from San Diego on Saturdays to Anaheim, where the car resides. Sometimes my husband, daughter, and best friend, Leslie Verfaillie, will come, and my dad will be there. I love to race and I love working on this car, but what I love most is doing those things with my family.

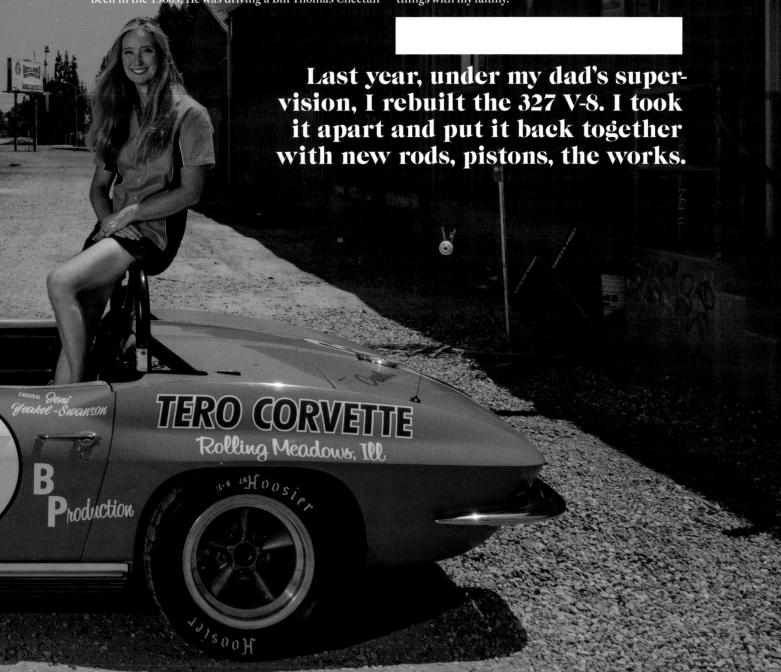

**Last year, under my dad's supervision, I rebuilt the 327 V-8. I took it apart and put it back together with new rods, pistons, the works.**

# A 1937 Cord 812 Phaeton from Indiana's "Little Detroit"

## Jim Weddle, sixty-four, the managing partner of Edward Jones, in St. Louis, MO

**FORTY-TWO YEARS AGO**, my wife Stacey and I moved to Connersville, Indiana, to open a branch office of the investment company Edward Jones. I had been an intern at the St. Louis headquarters while getting my MBA, and this was my first "real" job. I've been a car guy since I can remember, and what we found in Connersville was not just a great community, but what was to me an amazing automotive history.

In the 1920s and '30s, an industrialist named Errett Lobban (E.L.) Cord built Auburn and Duesenberg cars in Indiana. In 1929, he set out to build a car with his own name on it. Cord created a state-of-the-art car factory in Connersville to produce Cord and Auburn cars. Historians have called the small town Indiana's "Little Detroit."

When we moved there, my wife got a job at a company based in the old Cord assembly plant and you could see where the assembly line had once been.

Cord cars were luxurious and ahead of their time in terms of styling and engineering. Unfortunately, the Great Depression had a devastating effect on Indiana's auto business. Auburn, Duesenberg, and Cord all ended production during the Depression.

But the people of Indiana still celebrate these cars. We would see Cords at July 4th parades in Connersville, and I remember saying to my wife years ago, "Someday we are going to own one of those cars."

In 1984, we moved back to Edward Jones's headquarters in St. Louis. Ten years ago, my wife and I fulfilled our goal of purchasing a Cord. We found our 812 Phaeton through a classic car broker, for $200,000—top dollar, but it was one

**SPECS**

| Jim Weddle's Cord 812 Phaeton | |
| --- | --- |
| Engine: 289 cu in, V-8 | |
| Top speed: 90 mph | |
| Tires: Firestone | |

*Photography by Whitney Curtis*

## The car has front-wheel drive, retractable headlights controlled by cranks on either side of the dashboard, and a V-8 engine built by E.L. Cord's Lycoming company.

of the best I have seen. E.L. Cord envisioned this car to be a "baby Duesenberg." Coincidentally, our car was built during the final year of Cord's production.

The car has front-wheel drive, retractable headlights controlled by cranks on either side of the dashboard, and a V-8 engine built by E.L. Cord's Lycoming company. Our car had been restored before we bought it, and it is a delight to drive once you figure out its quirks. Our youngest son and his wife were driven from their wedding in our Cord, and our grandchildren love riding in the back seat with Gramps and Mimi.

Today, I have a collection of cars, but the Cord is a sentimental favorite. At the end of this year I will retire from Edward Jones, and traveling back to Connersville with this car is on my retirement bucket list.

# Ford Ranger Jewelry Repair Truck Offers a Home on the Road

**Claire Hummel, thirty-three, a jewelry designer and repair expert from San Francisco, CA**

**I INHERITED MY TRUCK** when my grandfather died four years ago. He lived in Missouri, and when he died, I drove the truck from St. Louis, where I grew up, to the West Coast. I remember thinking: Sorry, grandpa, I'm going to turn this truck into my traveling little home.

It started out as a simple gray pickup. I added the camper in the back, which I bought from a couple that custom-built it in the 1970s. Then I turned the truck into my room on wheels, a jewelry workshop, and also a place where I can keep things I've collected. As a jewelry maker, I create a lot of statement pieces, and my truck is its own statement piece. Everywhere I look in it, I see things that I love.

I have antiques from my grandfather, art pieces of all kinds made by people I've met and strangers too, textiles I've collected, memorabilia from my childhood, and tools that can fix anything. I keep my ring-sizers and sometimes solder torches in the truck, so I can repair jewelry or other things such as chandeliers, anywhere I go. I keep tons of blankets and utensils and my coffeemaker in the truck, too.

Basically, it has everything I could possibly need except a bathroom. I can stay in it for a month at a time while traveling and never miss home. Living in an urban environment for almost eleven years, the truck is like a getaway vehicle—an escape from the chaos.

I have a lot of vehicles, and I love them all: a bright turquoise 1964 Volkswagen Karmann Ghia, a large old Dodge work van, a small boat, and a small motorcycle. But my truck is my most beloved vehicle, and my daily driver.

I sometimes laugh thinking about what my grandfather would say if he could see the truck now. He'd be, like, what?! But I know he loves me. And he's happy his old Ford Ranger is still on the road and well taken care of.

> I sometimes laugh thinking about what my grandfather would say if he could see the truck now. He'd be, like, what?!

*Photography by Jason Henry*

**SPECS**

| | |
|---|---|
| Claire Hummel's Ford Ranger | |
| Engine: N/A | |
| Top speed: About 100 mph | |
| Tires: Goodyear | |

# A Sound Machine
# with Places to Go

**Steve Hwang, a member of music and art collective Space Cowboys, based in San Francisco, CA, and their 1973 Mercedes-Benz Unimog**

THE IDEA FOR THE MOG first came in 2000, and a lot of the original inspiration was Burning Man (an annual gathering in the Nevada desert). We wanted to create an urban assault vehicle that plays music, a fully self-contained mobile sound and video system.

We started with a 1973 Mercedes Unimog 404 that we got through an importer in Vallejo, California. The vehicle was originally created to be a military radio truck, and it's popular in the four-wheeling community because it has such high ground clearance and bullet-proof engineering. Once we had the truck, we started the build-out.

So many pitched in. Space Cowboys is a collective of people with many different talents—fabricating, sound engineering, mechanical expertise, and music production. When we started bringing the Mog to parties, it was pretty difficult. We had to tow speakers, generators, and other equipment in a second vehicle. My contribution was to make the Mog more plug-and-play. Everything is built in and, ideally, deploys at the push of a button.

We outfitted the truck with eight twenty-one-inch subwoofers in custom enclosures, and four all-weather stadium speakers mounted inside the cab that raise on a

SPECS

Space Cowboys' 1973 Mercedes-Benz Unimog 404 mobile sound system

Engine: Six-cylinder

Top speed: N/A

Tires: Continental

pneumatic lift. Concert-grade amplifiers, two seven-thousand-watt generators, a DJ booth—all of it is built in.

I manage the truck, and I've driven it to Burning Man, to gigs in Squaw Valley, Los Angeles, Santa Rosa, and all over the Bay Area. It's not your typical home-stereo setup. Our objective was to achieve a very high quality of sound, and to be able to take that quality sound wherever we want. We don't break any speed limits when we're on the road, but on flat pavement or moderate inclines, the Mog will cruise at 55 mph.

Needless to say, it's ground-shaking powerful. But our goal was never to be the biggest or loudest, or to compete with anyone. We just want to create our own sound, our own vibe, and to share it with our friends and our community. And mobility is a huge part of it.

## My contribution was to make the Mog more plug-and-play. Everything is built-in and, ideally, deploys at the push of a button.

**Steve Hwang and the Space Cowboys' sound system, built out of a 1973 Mercedes-Benz Unimog. It has a DJ booth and endless volume, and it is entirely mobile.**

# The Spirit of Rett:
## The Inspiration Behind
## a Land Speed Record

**Charlie Nearburg, sixty-five, president/owner of Nearburg Producing, based in Dallas, TX**

**MY SON RETT** was a wonderful person, and like his dad, a real gear head. Together we built motorcycles and raced cars, and we talked a lot about going to the Bonneville Salt Flats in Utah someday, the best place in the world to set land speed records. Rett fought a rare cancer for eleven years, and on January 14, 2005, it took his life at age twenty-one.

I spent a lot of time thinking about what to do in his

memory. I'd been interested in Bonneville since I was a kid, listening to the stories of the great salt-flat racers like Malcolm Campbell and the Summers brothers. In 2006, I bought a land-speed racing car from a gentleman in Los Angeles, and renamed it the Spirit of Rett. Then my crew and I set to work. In 2007, we made our first run at Bonneville. The car is a single-engine, normally aspirated car, and

**SPECS**

Charlie Nearburg's Spirit of Rett

Engine: 523 cu in, Reher-Morrison-built V-8

Top speed: 422.6 mph

Tires: Mickey Thompson

Charlie Nearburg named this car after his son Rett. Mr. Nearburg set a land speed record in the machine in 2010—over 414 mph. Pictured: Mr. Nearburg in his shop in Texas.

we were able to set two land speed records in our classes that first time out.

Over the years we changed the engine, transmission, nose design, everything but the overall shape. On September 21, 2010, the Spirit of Rett became the fastest single-engine, normally aspirated car in history—414.316 mph.

Land speed racing requires a tremendous amount of time and organization. The course on the salt flats is about three freeway lanes wide, and eleven miles long. Because of the curvature of the earth, you can't see the end from the start. Before a run, I walk the salt, then I stand where

I'm going to position the car at the start and pick a spot on a faraway mountain range, like I'm aiming a gun. When I'm traveling over four hundred miles per hour, I'm feeling everything the car is doing, working the throttle so I can put as much traction on the salt as I can, while maintaining my direction. To set a record, you have to run twice, and your speed is the average of the two. Slowing the car requires both brakes and a parachute.

It's an amazing sensation, feeling what engineering can do, and how fast I can go. We've recently rebuilt the Spirit of Rett. Our record still stands, but we're ready to roll again.

## To set a record, you have to run twice, and your speed is the average of the two. Slowing the car requires both brakes and a parachute.

# Was the 1936 Stout Scarab the Original Minivan?

**Ron Schneider, sixty-five, owner of Leon's Frozen Custard, of Milwaukee, WI**

WILLIAM B. STOUT was a Michigan-based inventor, best remembered for building the first all-metal airplane and a portable folding house, one of which I own. In the 1930s, he turned his attention to the auto industry with his Stout Scarab, of which nine were made.

His goal: to build a car of the future. It was no bigger than a normal car on the outside, with twice the room inside. It had flush window glass and fenders incorporated into the body, so it would drive without wind noise. It had a table, moving chairs, and three cigar lighters.

In retrospect, some say Stout built the first minivan. But the car, so radical and expensive for its time (about $5,000, which would be about $85,000 today), didn't catch on.

I paid $12,000 for one, and bought another for parts, then began a two-year restoration. Once done, I drove the Scarab across country twice. Along the way, I found Bill Stout's grandson, living in Phoenix. I asked if the car was like what he remembered as a boy. He said it was, down to the finger and nose prints on the windows, from people wanting to see inside.

Some thought Stout was a crackpot, at first. But his ideas were more right than wrong. I restored my Scarab to see if the car was as good as he said it was. And it is.

SPECS

Ron Schneider's 1936 Stout Scarab

Engine: Ford V-8

Top speed: Around 85 mph

Tires: Firestone

**In retrospect, some say Stout built the first minivan. But the car, so radical and expensive for its time . . . didn't catch on.**

*Photography by Sara Stathas*

# Once Controversial, This 1965 Chevrolet Corvair Monza Survives

### Christian Mejia, thirty-five, a property manager from Thousand Oaks, CA

**MY GRANDFATHER**, Dean Haskell, had a Corvair. When I was in preschool, he would take me to school in it. I thought it was the coolest car. When he passed away, he left it to my mom and when I got to high school, she gave it to me. It was my first car. That's when it all started. I have been obsessed with Corvairs ever since.

Chevrolet launched the Corvair in 1959 and it was unlike any car an American manufacturer had ever made. The engine was in the trunk, behind the driver. At the time, Volkswagen Beetles were very popular and the VW had its engine in the rear. Chevy wanted to tap into that market—

affordable, rear-engine cars. Soon there were Corvair coupes, sedans, station wagons, vans, even a pickup.

In the early 1960s these were popular cars. In 1964, however, the Ford Mustang came out, at about the same price, and that basically killed the Corvair. Also, at about that same time, Ralph Nader published a book called Unsafe at Any Speed, about how unsafe American cars were. The book made a special case of the Corvair. Ever since, the Corvair has had an infamous reputation. [A.J.: Nader wrote that the car's rear engine and suspension combination made it easy for drivers to lose control. Chevrolet changed

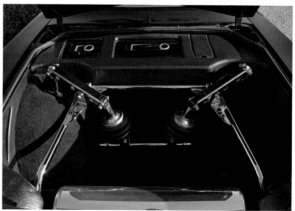

**Christian Mejia has owned twenty-six Corvairs. The black one pictured was his first; his grandfather used to drive him to school in this car, when he was a kid.**

*Photography by Ian Spanier*

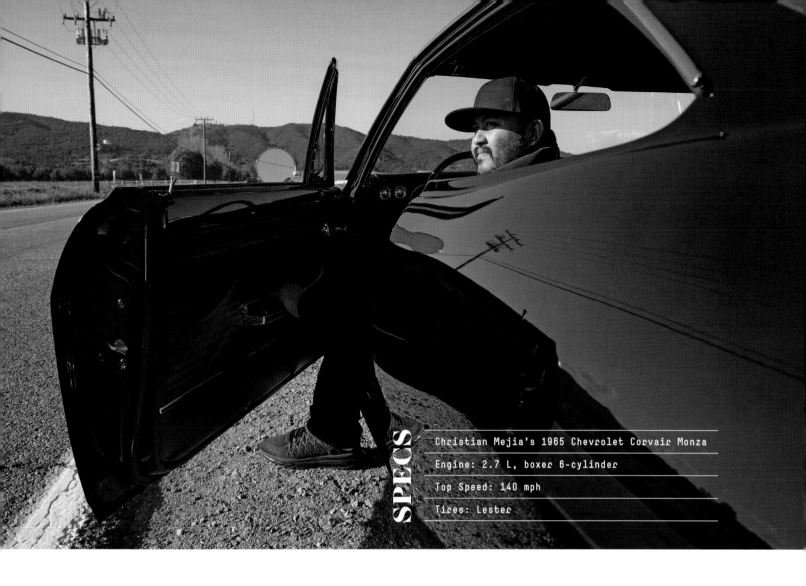

SPECS

Christian Mejia's 1965 Chevrolet Corvair Monza

Engine: 2.7 L, boxer 6-cylinder

Top Speed: 140 mph

Tires: Lester

the car's suspension setup due to Nader's book.]

I think that reputation is false because, to me, these cars handle so well. I am not alone. Today, there is a passionate community of Corvair people. These cars are unique and affordable, and people still use them to compete in vintage racing.

I have owned twenty-six Corvairs and currently own twelve, including two rare Corvair race cars, and I have my own private shop where I restore them. I have bought Corvairs in Arizona, New Mexico, Indiana, and California.

Once I was pulling a Corvair on a flatbed and I met a guy at a gas station. The next thing I knew, I was at his house in Barstow, California, and I bought five Corvairs for $3,000.

The car pictured here is my first Corvair, the one that my grandfather used to take me to preschool. I did some work on it: souped up the engine, did some body work, removed the door handles for a cleaner look, and swapped out the automatic transmission for a four-speed manual.

I know my grandfather would be proud, knowing his Corvair is still on the road.

**Chevy wanted to tap into that market—affordable, rear-engine cars. Soon there were Corvair coupes, sedans, station wagons, vans, even a pickup.**

# A Ride Back in Time in a 1940 Packard

### Nelson Bates, seventy-seven, an electrical engineer from Longview, TX

**ONE OF MY EARLIEST** memories is the time I was sitting in my uncle's Packard 110 at a family picnic where I grew up in West Virginia. I was seven years old, and my uncle let me play in the car, pretending I was driving it. I could hear a newscast from a portable radio that was sitting on a picnic table. It was August 6, 1945, and the newscast was talking about the atomic bomb that had just been dropped on Hiroshima. I still have that radio—an old Zenith.

Decades later, in 1997, I was in a hotel room when I saw an ad in a car magazine for a Packard for sale in Texas, where I have lived for many years. I went and saw the car three times before buying it, for $6,000. My brother and I began a restoration; we took the car apart, and my initial intuition was correct. This was the exact car my uncle owned, that I played in as a child.

My aunt had crashed the car, and the grille and some other pieces had been replaced. We found during our restoration that

## Packard was, in its day, the finest American car, in my opinion. I think of it as the American Rolls-Royce.

all the parts we suspected would not be original were in fact not, such as the grille and front fender. The car had a nameplate that listed Pringle as the dealership, in West Virginia. My uncle had purchased the car from that dealership, because the dealership belonged to his brother. All the facts lined up.

Packard was, in its day, the finest American car, in my opinion. I think of it as the American Rolls-Royce. The company was known for design and engineering, and the 110 was its lowest-priced car in 1940. Packard closed its factory in 1956, but not before it put out thousands of terrific automobiles.

The restoration on my 110 took four years. When it came time to paint it, I found an original Packard color sheet from 1940. My wife picked out the paint: Laguna Maroon. When we drive the car now, it doesn't feel like we're going back in time. It feels almost like a modern car, because in my opinion, this Packard was way ahead of its time.

**SPECS**

Nelson Bates's 1940 Packard

Engine: 245 cu in, 6-cylinder

Top speed: Over 100 mph

Tires: Lester 16 x 6.50

SPECS

Gerard Pfeffer's 1989 Geo Metro "Outlaw Street Car"

Engine: 465 cu in, V-8

Top speed: 157 mph

Tires: Hoosier

# A Humble Geo, Souped Up for Drag Racing

### Gerard Pfeffer, a sheet-metal worker from St. Louis, MO, and his 1989 Geo Metro "Outlaw Street Car"

IN 1995, MY FRIEND, the late Bobby Kruse, and I decided to build an outlaw streetcar. We had been tinkering with engines together most of our lives, and we wanted to build something no one else ever had. When it came to cars, there was nothing Bobby could not do. One day he called and asked me if I was sitting down.

"I've got our car," he said. "A Geo Metro." I said, "What?!?" The truth was, we did not have much money, and Bobby's boss gave him a Geo for free. So a Geo Metro it would be. [A.J: The Geo Metro was a joint venture between General Motors and Suzuki, from model years 1989 to 1997.]

It took us two years to build the car. Almost nothing is stock, except the body, the dashboard, and the seats, and almost all the components came from local speed shops in the St. Louis area. Bobby and I were getting clean and sober, and these were two of the most inspiring years of my life. We worked night and day, and we would never let each other down.

The night we finished the car in 1997, we took it out to put fuel in it. When people saw it, they were saying: What

## When people saw it, they were saying: What kind of sick minds build a street dragster out of a Geo Metro?

kind of sick minds build a street dragster out of a Geo Metro?

But the Geo earned itself a reputation in St. Louis. It was quite a spectacle at car shows, and Bobby hit furious speeds on the drag strip the first time out, roughly doubling the highway speed limit in the space of a quarter mile. When I look at pictures of us back then, Bobby and I are always smoking cigars and laughing.

In 2001, Bobby was killed in a motorcycle crash. The car ended up in my basement, packed in mothballs. It stayed there for thirteen years, until I could gather the money to put it back on the street. It's been running again for one year, as of this month [A.J.: This article originally was published on October 18, 2016], with a new big-block Chevy motor built by a Missouri speed shop called Dasco Racing Engines.

Ever since Bobby died, I set my alarm to 8:08 on the days I'm off, because, in digital numbers, that spells Bob. I'm just happy to have this car back on the road, in honor of my fallen friend.

The MG TD was one of the first European sports cars to gain popularity in America. Pictured: Jon Shuler and his wife, Cynthia, with the 1952 model they bought over fifty years ago.

SPECS

Jon Shuler's 1952 MG TD

Engine: 1.25 L, inline 4-cylinder

Top Speed: 60 mph (downhill!)

Tires: N/A

*Photography by Rachel Shuler*

# A 1952 MG Gets to Join
# the West Point Reunion

### Jon Shuler, an Anglican priest from Pawleys Island, SC

**FOR MORE YEARS** than I can remember, I have had a fantasy brewing in my mind. My wife Cynthia and I would drive our MG TD to West Point, New York for my fiftieth reunion at the United States Military Academy. [A.J.: This article originally appeared in the Wall Street Journal on March 28, 2017.] We were married the day after I graduated, in 1967. This was the car we drove through the gates at West Point after graduation, to go on our honeymoon.

My plan has been to put a sign on the vehicle: "Same Car, Same Wife, Same Weight."

This May, that dream will come true, though I will have to put an asterisk next to the word "weight." I still weigh the same, but the pounds have been redistributed.

I first saw an MG TD when I was in the eighth grade. I thought, "Man, if I could ever own one of those cars someday." The British-built MG T-series had a huge impact on the history of cars. It was one of the first European sports cars to arrive in the U.S., in the years after World War II, and it helped spark a passion for sports cars that remains with us today.

I bought mine my senior year at West Point, for $1,500. It was a lot of money. My dad fronted me $700, and Cynthia and I had the other $800. We named the car Hannah, after an old relative of mine. For many years, my MG sat languishing in my garage. In 2003, I began a restoration. It is an expensive endeavor, and I had to nickel-and-dime my way through. In September of 2016, the finished car arrived home.

When I was twenty-two, I would drive this car everywhere. My wife and I drove it to my first job, in Kentucky. I drove it to Texas, and to New York twice. If the car had any trouble, I would push it to the side of the road and fix it. Now that I'm seventy-one, it's a little more anxiety-provoking. It strains to get up to sixty miles per hour, but at about fifty-five, it purrs like a sewing machine.

It will be a great moment, to drive onto the West Point campus with Cynthia. The car has always been a symbol of our happy marriage. We have three children, and this car feels like a fourth.

## It will be a great moment, to drive onto the West Point campus with Cynthia. The car has always been a symbol of our happy marriage.

SPECS

| | |
|---|---|
| Tina Dillard-Eisner's 1982 Datsun 280ZX | |
| Engine: 2.8 L, inline 6-cylinder | |
| Top Speed: Over 120 mph | |
| Tires: BF Goodrich | |

# The Ultimate Police Cruiser: A 1982 Datsun 280ZX

## Tina Dillard-Eisner, a sergeant with a metro Atlanta, GA, police department

GROWING UP, I ALWAYS LOVED Z CARS. I loved the long hood and the taillights, particularly on the 1982 and 1983 models. I used to wear a T-shirt that said "280ZX Fan" on the back—white with orange sleeves. Orange and blue were my high school colors, so I wore the shirt with blue jeans on school-spirit days.

The Z car became a huge phenomenon starting in the 1970s, a Japanese sports car that took the world by storm. For years I dreamed of owning one, but I was paying my way through school and could not afford one. Every time I saw a Z, I'd point and say, "Beauty baby!" I kept an album full of pictures I took of Z cars that I saw on the street.

On September 1, 1991, I was on patrol working the late-night shift when I responded to an alarm at a Ford dealership in Decatur, Georgia. We get a lot of false alarms, but if it's a business late at night, it's more likely there's an actual burglary going on. Turns out, it was a false alarm,

but while I was checking the place out, I saw this 280ZX in the lot, for sale. I said to myself: Beauty baby!

It was orange, the same color as the sleeves of my high school spirit Z car T-shirt (which I still have). It was a 1982, my favorite Z year. I was thinking: Why is this Datsun for sale at this Ford dealership? Surely I was meant to meet this car. I bought it the next day. It needed a facelift and new paint, and the paint job cost more than the car did.

I have now owned it for twenty-five years, and have had many adventures. The night I met my husband in 1993, we rode together in this car. I lost one of my best friends to a motorcycle accident, and just before, we rode in this car. So when I drive it now, I feel his presence. And yes, I have measured how fast this car can go.

For some, cars are for getting to work and running errands. This car, for me, is a dream come true.

**Going back to the 1970s, Japanese Z cars have been a sales phenomenon, an affordable and reliable vehicle with classic sports car styling—long nose, short rear deck.**

**Why is this Datsun for sale at this Ford dealership? Surely I was meant to meet this car. I bought it the next day.**

SPECS

| | |
|---|---|
| Dave Gano's 1931 Cadillac Limousine | |
| Engine: 452 cu in, V-16 | |
| Top speed: About 85 mph | |
| Tires: Firestone | |

# The Gatsby-esque Grandeur of a 1931 Cadillac Limousine

## Dave Gano, of Salem, OH

**CARS CAN BE REMARKABLE** time capsules. In the 1920s—an era of unparalleled Wall Street success—companies like Cadillac, Lincoln, and Duesenberg were vying to become the preeminent maker of American luxury cars. My Cadillac 452A Fleetwood Imperial Limousine was built after the stock market crash, but it's really an emblem of the roaring 1920s.

The size alone communicates Gatsby-esque grandeur. The car cost about $6,500 new, according to my research, at a time when a new Chevy could cost under $500, and it weighs well over 6,000 pounds—more than the biggest Cadillac Escalade available today.

It's meant to be chauffeur-driven. The front seats are all original black leather, and there's a case with Cadillac-supplied maps of every state, as the roads looked at the time. A glass divider window can close off the front compartment from the rear.

In back, the car's owner had all imaginable luxuries, all of which are still in the car: a sterling silver cigarette case with a beveled-glass mirror, an intercom system that allows a passenger to talk to the driver through a microphone, and silk blinds on the windows. I have been told by professional cabinet makers that some of the interior's detail is as finely crafted as any furniture they've seen.

The engine is a huge 452-cubic-inch, sixteen-cylinder, built to make very little noise. When you rev it, you hear mostly the sound of air going into the carburetors.

When I was young, my father and I restored old Cadillacs together, and I had planned when I bought this one in 2013 to just get it roadworthy. But after twenty-two months of restoration, I started showing the car. This August, it won third place in its class at the Pebble Beach Concours d'Elegance, the most important classic car show in the world. Even to be invited was a great honor.

Not that it's just a show car. Earlier this month, my wife and I drove 1,200 miles through New England, and the car ran perfectly (about 6.5 miles per gallon). Next spring, I'm planning to use it as my daily driver—no chauffeur needed.

**In the 1920s into the early '30s, Cadillac was competing with Duesenberg and Lincoln to be the preeminent builder of luxury cars in America. Pictured is Dave Gano's 1931 Cadillac limo.**

**I have been told by professional cabinet makers that some of the interior's detail is as finely crafted as any furniture they've seen.**

# The 2007 Hyundai Accent of the World's Coldest Pizza Man

## Aleksandar Joksic, twenty-five, co-owner of East Coast Pizzeria in Barrow, AK

**BARROW IS THE MOST NORTHERN** town in the U.S., above the Arctic Circle. There are three pizzerias, but ours is the only one that specializes only in delivery.

The busiest season is winter because nobody wants to go outside. It's dark, and the temperature hits minus-40 degrees Fahrenheit. At certain times, it's normal to see a polar bear in the middle of the street. A large pepperoni pie costs $18, and we have special bags to keep the food warm.

Four months ago, we bought a used 2007 Hyundai Accent for deliveries. Gas costs over $6 a gallon in Barrow, and the Hyundai is very economical. Every morning first thing I start the car (it takes an hour to get up to temperature) and unplug it (an electric mechanism keeps the engine and fluids from freezing at night). If I turn it off for ten minutes, it would freeze and die, so I don't turn it off until the end of the day.

When delivering, I wear huge boots, three pairs of specially made Eskimo socks, two pairs of pants, three hoodies, and a very big jacket. I park very close to the restaurant, so I'm not outside for long. I keep a heater on inside the car day and night, so the window glass doesn't break.

Almost every day in winter, I get stuck somewhere. I'm young; it's an adventure.

**SPECS**

| Aleksandar Joksic's 2007 Hyundai Pizza Delivery Machine | |
| --- | --- |
| Engine: 1.6 L, 4-cylinder | |
| Top speed: N/A | |
| Tires: N/A | |

*Photography by Mark Meyer*

**While delivering pizza in this 2007 Hyundai, says Aleksandar Joksic, it is not rare to see a polar bear crossing the road.**

# I was in total disbelief. He still had the car, only it had been sitting behind his shop for about 30 years.

The 356 was Porsche's very first production model, introduced in 1948. This one, owned by Jim Doughton in Florida, has a story unlike any other.

**SPECS**

Jim Doughton's 1953 Porsche 356 Cabriolet

Engine: 1.5 L, boxer 4-cylinder

Top Speed: 99 mph

Tires: Kumho

# A Vintage Porsche
## Returns, Fifty Years Later

**Jim Doughton, a regional newspaper publisher with GateHouse Media
from Gainesville, FL, and his 1953 Porsche 356 Cabriolet**

**I WAS RAISED BY** a single mother who drove hand-me-down Chevrolets. Growing up in St. Petersburg, Florida, I had an infatuation with European sports cars. I saved all my money and before I left for college in 1969, I bought a 1953 Porsche 356 Cabriolet for $500.

The 356 was Porsche's very first production model, introduced in 1948 and first imported to the U.S. in the early 1950s. In the late 1960s, these were not expensive cars. Mine had blown its Porsche engine so it had a VW motor in it. I drove that car during college, then sold it to a guy who worked at a hippie store called the Subterranean Circus in Gainesville, Florida. I never remembered his name. What did it matter?

Four decades later, I ended up in Gainesville. I decided to buy a 356 again. The passion for that body style never left me. Someone tipped me off that a local guy who ran a body shop called GT Motorcars had one. So I showed up and met the owner, Bob Sturm. I told him I had once owned a 356 years earlier, and had sold it to a guy who worked at the Subterra-nean Circus in Gainesville.

He said, "I worked at Subterranean Circus." He asked about the car's color and I said silver. He said, "Are you from St. Petersburg?" I said yeah. He said, "You sold that car to me."

I was in total disbelief. He still had the car, only it had been sitting behind his shop for about thirty years, chained to an oak tree. He was not keen on selling. I was thinking, "How am I going to get this car back?" It took convincing.

In 2005, I traded an antique motorcycle plus some money (not a lot) for my old 356. The car was in bad shape—if it had sat outside for one more year, it might've been lost forever. Mr. Sturm's shop helped me with a three-year restoration. During that time, I saw another Porsche painted Guard's Red and it looked so good, I had my car painted that color. I put a 1961 Porsche engine in it, and it can do seventy-five miles per hour all day long.

Never in my wildest dreams could I imagine I would be driving the same car I drove while in college, fifty years later.

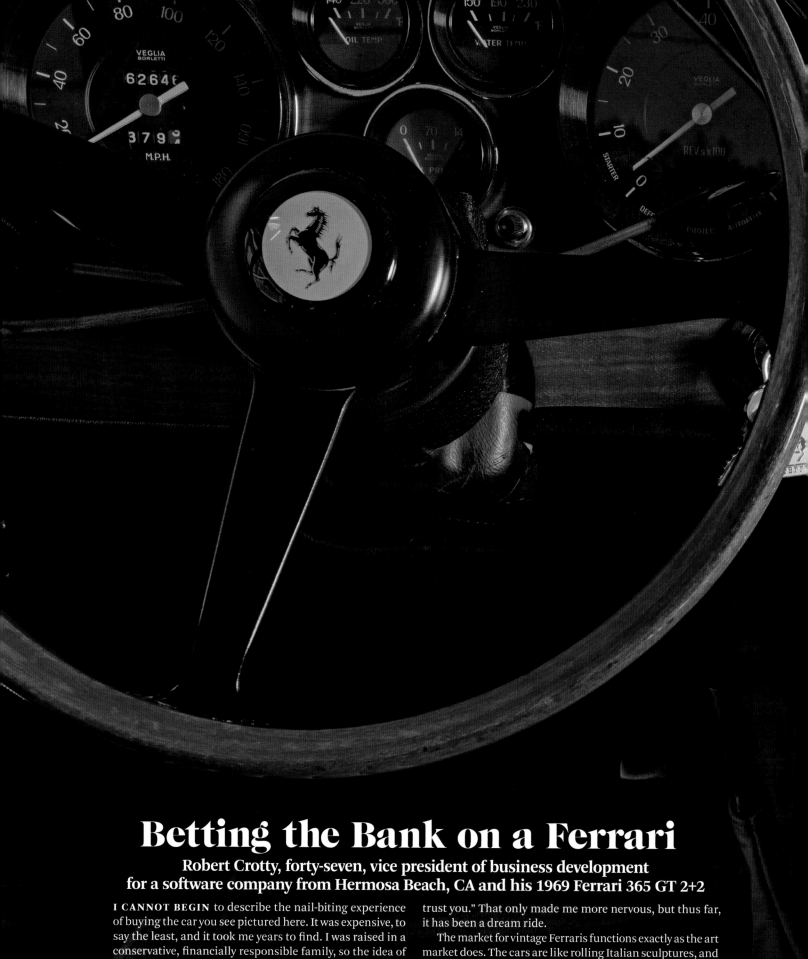

# Betting the Bank on a Ferrari

**Robert Crotty, forty-seven, vice president of business development
for a software company from Hermosa Beach, CA and his 1969 Ferrari 365 GT 2+2**

**I CANNOT BEGIN** to describe the nail-biting experience of buying the car you see pictured here. It was expensive, to say the least, and it took me years to find. I was raised in a conservative, financially responsible family, so the idea of tying up my family's financial well-being in a car was, let's say, surprising to some people. When I bought the car in 2013, my wife said to me, "Whatever you think is right. I

trust you." That only made me more nervous, but thus far, it has been a dream ride.

The market for vintage Ferraris functions exactly as the art market does. The cars are like rolling Italian sculptures, and their values fluctuate according to the ebb and flow of desire for specific models, the rarity and provenance, etc. Buyers and collectors usually have one of two motives: They buy a car

SPECS

Robert Crotty's 1969 Ferrari 365 GT 2+2

Engine: 4.4 L, V-12

Top Speed: 152 mph

Tires: Michelin

This 1969 Ferrari 365 GT 2+2—owned by Robert Crotty—is from the so-called Enzo era, back when company founder Enzo Ferrari owned the company entirely.

because they know it has monetary value and is likely to appreciate, or they have the money and they just want to enjoy it.

I fall in the middle. Driving this car is a surreal experience—the beauty, the sound, the power. But I also need the car to maintain its value, and ideally to appreciate. (Thus far, I believe it has.) I chose this specific model because it was affordable (for my budget), I could fit my family in it, and because it was one of the last V-12 cars—Ferraris are famous for the V-12 engine—during the so-called Enzo era. That's when founder Enzo Ferrari owned the company entirely, before it was partly sold to Fiat in 1969. About eight hundred of these cars were built.

The company was really an extension of Enzo Ferrari's passion. He was incredibly successful in racing, and there's an aura about his road cars because of the beauty and engineering brilliance he instilled in them.

I look for any excuse I can to put my family in the car and go. I take my kids for night drives. Sometimes before they go to bed, we jump in the Ferrari and blast through the neighborhood. Taking them for ice cream has never been so much fun.

The kids point out how loud the car is, and how the air conditioning doesn't work that well. I tell them, "Well, kids, welcome to 1960s motoring."

# The kids point out how loud the car is, and how the air conditioning doesn't work that well. I tell them, "Well, kids, welcome to 1960s motoring."

# Time Travel in a 1970 Chevrolet Corvette Stingray

## Jason Laureys, forty, a Southwest Airlines pilot from Wauconda, IL

WHEN I WAS LITTLE, instead of a stuffed animal, I slept with toy trucks and Matchbox cars. By the time I was in junior high, because I loved cars so much, my parents had taught me to drive. We had a family friend whose husband owned a 1979 Corvette, and she let me drive it through my neighborhood.

I did not have a license yet. I remember sitting in that driver's seat, looking out over those huge swooping fenders. In that moment, everything changed.

Today I have three Corvettes and two Camaros. The car pictured here is a third-generation ("C3") Corvette, like the one I drove when I was in junior high, and it has a special story.

I bought it in June 2015 from a mom-and-pop dealership in Chicago for $32,195. I was given a file that had history on the car. Last year I took the vehicle to a car show in the town next to mine. This guy comes up and starts taking pictures. He tells me he used to own a Corvette just like mine, in the 1970s into the early '80s.

The more we talked, the more it clicked. All the history I had on my car, this guy was now telling me. He had lived in Colorado when he owned his Corvette, and I knew my car had once resided in Colorado. Same color, same model year, same 454 390-horsepower engine. His name was Dale Seay and he gave me his number. I was thinking: What are the chances this is the same car this stranger had owned decades ago, in a different state?

That night, I searched through the file I had on the car and found a service receipt from 1975 that had Dale Seay's name on it. I was flabbergasted.

A week later I brought the car to him and let him drive it. I love hearing his stories from the 1970s, how he used to speed the car through rural Colorado where there were no police, and how when he drove his daughter to school, all the boys would go nuts over the Corvette.

He's seventy-nine, and I'm forty, but we share the car in common. Watching him drive it today is almost as much fun as driving it myself.

**SPECS**

Jason Laureys's 1970 Chevrolet Corvette Stingray

Engine: 7.4 L, V-8

Top Speed: About 145 mph

Tires: BF Goodrich

Two men who have owned this same Corvette, Jason Laureys (left, the current owner),
and Dale Seay, who owned the car from the 1970s into the early '80s.

Kentucky-based oncologist Dr. John Gohmann uses this 1953 Kaiser for his commute to work.
The trip, he says, is a "marvelous window of serenity."

# A 1953 Kaiser Dragon Serves as a History Lesson

### Dr. John Gohmann, sixty-two, an oncologist from Lexington, KY

**EVERY MORNING, I DRIVE** two and a half miles to work in the Dragon. The car was born the same year as I was. It's almost outrageously 1950s-ish, and unbelievably slow, which is just fine with me. It turns my commute into a marvelous window of serenity.

When I bought the car, I knew nothing about the man who'd built it. Henry Kaiser was a very talented and driven individual, and to some degree, he's been lost to history. The Dragon's steering wheel has four postage-stamp-size emblems on it, and together, they tell his story.

There's a dam (Kaiser's company built the Hoover Dam during the Great Depression), a ship (due to his production of Liberty ships during World War II, Kaiser is known as the father of modern American ship building), a factory (for his mass-production prowess), and of course, a car.

Kaiser only built passenger cars from 1947 to 1955 in the U.S., and the Dragon was the top-of-the-line model in 1953. He was also instrumental in starting Kaiser Permanente, today one of the biggest medical conglomerates in the country.

My particular car sat in a museum for twenty years before I bought it at an auction, so it's in terrific condition. There's no air conditioning, the AM radio doesn't work, and it has a ridiculous name, but it has a distinct personality that I love.

## My particular car sat in a museum for 20 years before I bought it at an auction, so it's in terrific condition.

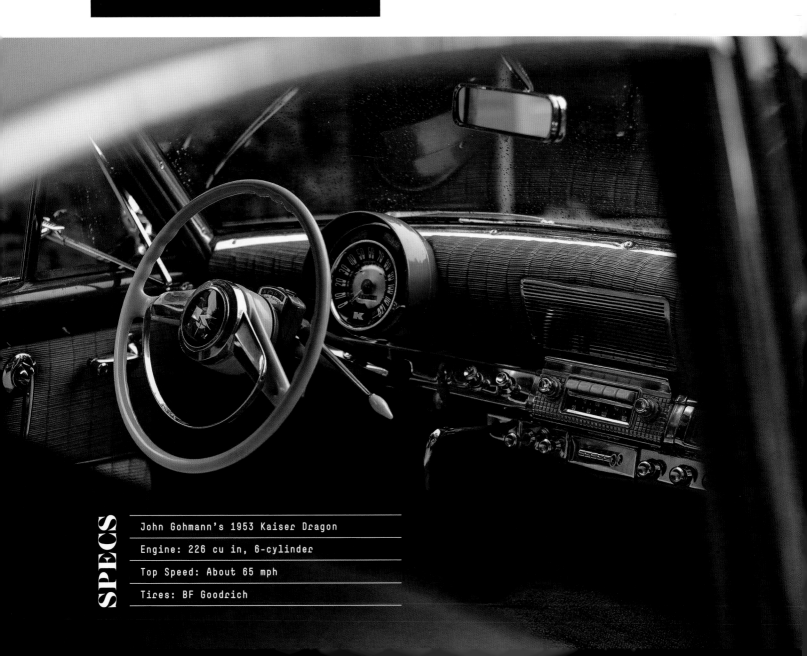

**SPECS**

| | |
|---|---|
| John Gohmann's 1953 Kaiser Dragon | |
| Engine: 226 cu in, 6-cylinder | |
| Top Speed: About 65 mph | |
| Tires: BF Goodrich | |

In the 1960s, Allen Grant was a professional racing driver. He has owned this incredibly rare Lola since that era, and has only driven the car once.

## Lo-Lo-Lo-Lola
**The obscure maker of the car pictured here went on to build sick Indy 500 vehicles. And the winners are . . .**

1. 1966 Indy 500 winner, driver Graham Hill, Mecom Racing, Ford engine, average speed 144.317 mph

2. 1978 Indy 500 winner, driver Al Unser, Chaparral Racing, Cosworth engine, average speed 161.363 mph

3. 1990 Indy 500 winner, driver Arie Luyendyk, Shierson Racing, Chevrolet engine, average speed 185.981 mph

*Photography by Ray Ewing*

# A 1963 Lola GT Mk6:
# Too Classic to Drive

## Allen Grant, seventy-five, a real-estate developer from La Quinta, CA

**THE CAR YOU SEE HERE** is so rare and meaningful to me, I have owned it for fifty-one years, and I have driven it once. I'll get to that in a moment.

In 1963, the Lola GT made a dramatic debut at the London Racing Car Show. I read about it in magazines, which I still own. It was the prettiest car I had ever seen, and it was revolutionary.

Designed by a British engineer named Eric Broadley, it stood only forty inches tall and had an affordable American V-8 engine (a Ford) just behind the cockpit. Today, it is known as the inspiration for the Ford GT40, one of the most iconic racing cars ever. At the time, only three Lola GTs were built.

In 1965, I was working as a racing driver and mechanic for Carroll Shelby, in England. [A.J.: The Shelby American racing team won the GT world championship that year.] Our shop was next to Lola's. I saw one of these Lola GTs and negotiated to buy it for $3,000—a lot of money for me at the time, especially since the car had no engine in it.

It was the prototype, the first Lola GT built.

Over fifty years, this car followed me around as I moved from place to place. I was building a business and did not have time for much else. But I promised I would someday mount an engine in the Lola and restore it to the exact specifications of how it appeared when I first saw pictures of it at the 1963 London Racing Car Show.

With the help of friends, I finished the car. I had an engine builder craft a period-correct 1960s Ford V-8. In August, I trailered the car to an event called The Quail, A Motorsports Gathering, at the Monterey Car Week in California.

People who knew what this car was could not believe their eyes. The Lola won an award, and to accept it, I had to drive it onto a stage. It was the first and only time I've driven this car, a truly amazing moment.

Already, I have invitations to bring this automobile to shows all over the globe. So that's what I am going to do—travel the world with my Lola.

## I had to drive it onto a stage. It was the first and only time I've driven this car, a truly amazing moment.

**SPECS**

| Allen Grant's Lola GT Mk6 |
| --- |
| Engine: Ford 289 cu in, V-8 |
| Top Speed: About 185 mph |
| Tires: Dunlop |

# Picking Up the Pieces of a Classic Truck

### Kurt Stocker, eighty, an artist from Corrales, NM, and his 1954 International Harvester R-120 Pickup

**IN 2009 I WAS LIVING IN** Westcliffe, Colorado, a town so small the whole population could fit on a 747. Driving home I used to pass this crapped-out pickup with a "for sale" sign, sitting in a field. I finally called the number and agreed to a price on one condition: The owner could drive the truck to my ranch, which was up nasty roads at nine thousand feet elevation. The truck made the trip, so I wrote a check for $1,700.

I admit: I am not a smart man. A smart man would have bought an old Ford or Chevy. Finding parts so I could restore this International Harvester was exceedingly difficult, but it became my obsession.

To do the work, I partnered with the guy in my small town who did all the maintenance on local school buses. I remember calling a guy in Colorado who supposedly had a 1954 R-120 bumper. He said, "You'll have to wait until the snow melts. I think there's one lying in my field." After nearly two years, the job was done, and I used

**SPECS**

Kurt Stocker's 1954 International Harvester R-120

Engine: 220 cu in, inline 6-cylinder

Top Speed: 42 mph ["So far," says Mr. Stocker.]

Tires: N/A

# Driving home I used to pass this crapped-out pickup with a "for sale" sign, sitting in a field.

the truck to do what it was born to do: hard work.

Most people today have never heard of International Harvester, but for a large part of the twentieth century, it was probably the brand for ranch and farm equipment in the Midwest, and the company made pickups, too. [A.J.: According to a 1953 Wall Street Journal article, International Harvester was the third-biggest producer of pickup trucks that year, behind Chevrolet and Ford.] Until it hit hard times in the 1980s, International Harvester was one of the brands that helped make this country what it is today.

My truck has its original straight-six engine. It has something called a granny low—a first gear that moves the vehicle about three miles per hour, walking speed, so you can get out of the truck and it'll move along by itself while you are, say, loading the bed with hay. It also has tremendous torque, so it can pull stumps out of the ground.

I have since moved from Colorado, and the vehicle is no longer a work truck. I use it to drive my grandkids through the desert, along the Rio Grande. The truck was built the year I graduated high school, and it is certainly a step back in time.

# The Ballad of Speedy Cop
# & the Gang of Outlaws

### Jeff Bloch, a Washington, D.C., police sergeant, and his Lemons racing cars

**I HAVE BEEN A POLICE OFFICER** for twenty-two years, and I have been racing cars longer than that. I first heard about 24 Hours of Lemons racing in 2009. (Lemons, which recently changed its name from LeMons, is a pun on a bad car and the 24 Hours of Le Mans, regarded as the world's most important sports car race.) It's a nationwide endurance racing series, and at the same time, a contest for who can make the coolest, most absurd racing car. I am overly competitive, but I'm also forty-four going on eight. This was for me.

I put together a team called Speedycop & the Gang of Outlaws. My wife Jaime is outlaw #1 and the rest is an eclectic mix. I do the design and engineering. We build the vehicles in my garage, and we race them. In Lemons racing, it does not matter as much who is fastest but who wins the prize for coolest fast car—the Index of Effluency prize. We have won nine times.

Our latest is the Trippy Tippy Hippy Van. We took the body a 1976 Volkswagen bus, flipped it on its side, slid a 1988 Volkswagen Rabbit into it, and built it into a race car, so you cannot see the Rabbit, only the sideways van. Lemons cars have to cost no more than $500; after you have the base vehicle you can spend as much as you want making it cool. I found a Rabbit in Texas for $500, and the build took five intense weeks. Then we raced in Kentucky (the vehicle can hit about 100 miles per hour), winning the Index of Effluency award.

Other cars include Speedy's Weenies—a hot-dog stand welded onto a Suzuki SUV. (At a race earlier this year in New Jersey, we came in forty-eighth out of 124, which means we beat over seventy-five cars—in a hot-dog stand.) There's the Spirit of LeMons (an abandoned 1956 airplane body mounted onto a 1987 Toyota), and the Upside Down Camaro (the name says it all). The SpeedyCopter is a Vietnam-era attack helicopter body mounted on a 1986 Toyota. We built this vehicle to be amphibious, so after I raced it, I drove it on a lake on propeller power.

My wife is a saint. We have two incomes and no kids, and we scratch by because everything goes into racing. On the track, we drive these cars hard, and we have an absolute blast.

I put together a team called Speedycop &
the Gang of Outlaws. My wife Jaime is
outlaw #1 and the rest is an eclectic mix.

Jeff Bloch and his wife, Jaime, build bizarre cars to race in the 24 Hours of Lemons.
The Volkswagen van is called the Trippy Tippy Hippy Van, and it can hit about one hundred miles per hour.

# Steam Power Meets the Twenty-First Century

### Curt Brohard, sixty-four, a dentist from Walnut Creek, CA, and his 1906 Stanley Model H

GROWING UP IN the San Francisco Bay Area, my brother Allan and I used to visit a cabin near Lake Tahoe with our family, and on the property, there was an old car sort of melting into the ground. Many years later my brother started restoring old cars, and we took a closer look at this automobile, which was still sitting in the same place. We realized it was a rare 1906 Stanley Model H—a steam-powered car.

The descendants of the owner of this car had documentation of an extraordinary story. A man named Edward Chamberlain bought it in 1915 to take his bride on a honeymoon, from Oakland to Yosemite National Park—no small feat, on the primitive roads of the time. On returning, he left the car at a family cabin near Lake Tahoe, where it sat for many decades.

Stanley cars were built by F.E. and F.O. Stanley, two brothers, until the mid-1920s, at a factory in Newton, Massachusetts. The year this Stanley was built (1906), the Stanley steamer became the fastest car in existence, when a Stanley factory racer set a world speed record of over 127 miles per hour.

The 1906 Stanley runs on steam, just like a steam locomotive. Owner Curt Brohard, above, spent twenty years restoring this car with his brother Allan.

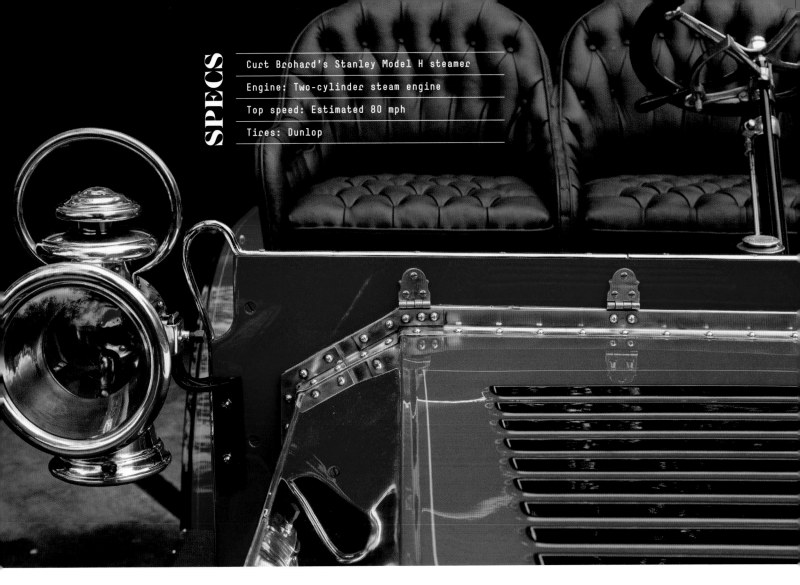

SPECS

| | |
|---|---|
| Curt Brohard's Stanley Model H steamer | |
| Engine: | Two-cylinder steam engine |
| Top speed: | Estimated 80 mph |
| Tires: | Dunlop |

My brother and I bought the old Stanley in 1996 from Edward Chamberlain's descendants for $2,000. We began a twenty-year restoration, which we finished in fall of 2016. The job was laborious, to say the least. Since the car had been sitting for eighty years, we used a metal detector to hunt for all the original existing pieces we could find. Many other parts we had to fabricate from scratch.

What is a steam-powered car? There's a burner under a boiler, which turns water into steam. The steam is piped into the engine, and the expansion of the steam is what pushes the pistons back and forth, just like in a steam locomotive. [A.J.: Stanley cars have no relation to the Stanley steam carpet-cleaning company of today.]

We have sought to make our car exactly as it was when it rolled out of the Stanley Motor Carriage Co. factory 111 years ago. We believe our 1906 Stanley Model H is the only one of its kind, accurately restored to its original specifications, in the world.

# We believe our 1906 Stanley Model H is the only one of its kind, accurately restored to its original specifications, in the world.

By all accounts, the Audi R8 is a triumph of design, and thus it is a natural fit
for Kerby Jean-Raymond, founder of the fashion label Pyer Moss.

SPECS

Kerby Jean-Raymond's 2009 Audi R8

Engine: 4.2 L, V-8

Top Speed: Estimated 187 mph

Tires: N/A

# Taking a Chance on a 2009 Audi R8

**Kerby Jean-Raymond, twenty-nine, the New York–based founder of fashion label Pyer Moss**

**I WAS GOING THROUGH A BREAKUP** at the time. My girlfriend had left and taken our Jeep, and I was really mad. I ended up looking at cars on eBay when I saw this Audi R8. I have always had a passion for Audis. The R8, if you're an Audi fan, is the car. I bid on it, and when my bid got accepted, I was like: Oh crap, what have I done?!

I got the car for a great price, but it was definitely an impulse buy. I was taking out loans to get my business going; I worried about how I was going to pay for the car, and what kind of condition it would be in.

It arrived in New York from California in April 2015, and the guy from the trucking company who handed me the keys was a rough-looking dude. The car had an inch of brown soot on it. When I opened the door, so much dirt fell off, it felt like snow. I started it up and drove directly to my family's home in Queens. My nieces, my nephews—everyone gathered around the car. This kind of a car was a first for my family, and it was a great moment. All it needed was a good wash, and it was ready to roll.

When people see the R8, they tell me it looks like me. I wanted black on black, because I always wear black. I love the lines—the low profile, the angular headlights, the way the car looks like it's going fast even when it's standing still. It's sporty and sleek, like the way I try to draw my leather jackets and sweatpants. You don't find a lot of daily driving cars that can convey that kind of style, at this price range. I wanted the automatic and not a manual, because driving an automatic in the city is so much easier.

I've since reconciled with my girlfriend, and I let her drive the car. I was already thinking about what I might get next, but she said no way. We're keeping this one.

> **My nieces, my nephews—everyone gathered around the car. This kind of a car was a first for my family, and it was a great moment.**

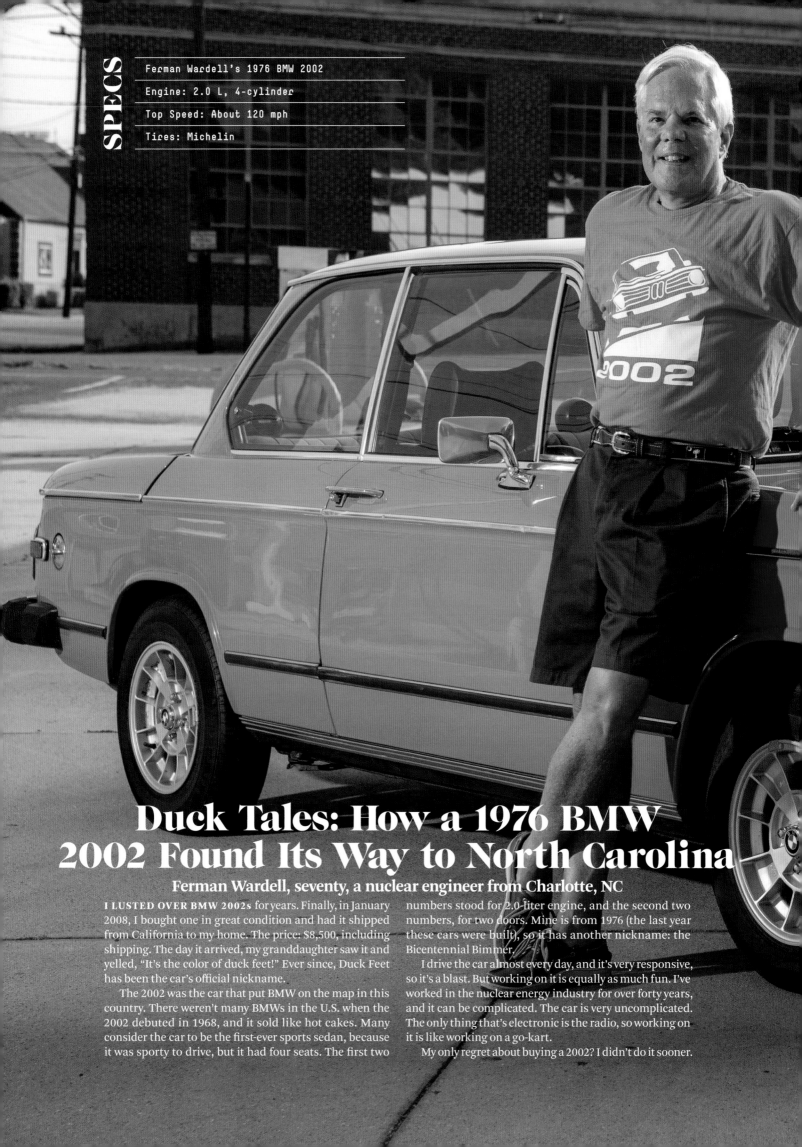

**SPECS**

Ferman Wardell's 1976 BMW 2002

Engine: 2.0 L, 4-cylinder

Top Speed: About 120 mph

Tires: Michelin

# Duck Tales: How a 1976 BMW 2002 Found Its Way to North Carolina

### Ferman Wardell, seventy, a nuclear engineer from Charlotte, NC

**I LUSTED OVER BMW 2002s** for years. Finally, in January 2008, I bought one in great condition and had it shipped from California to my home. The price: $8,500, including shipping. The day it arrived, my granddaughter saw it and yelled, "It's the color of duck feet!" Ever since, Duck Feet has been the car's official nickname.

The 2002 was the car that put BMW on the map in this country. There weren't many BMWs in the U.S. when the 2002 debuted in 1968, and it sold like hot cakes. Many consider the car to be the first-ever sports sedan, because it was sporty to drive, but it had four seats. The first two

numbers stood for 2.0-liter engine, and the second two numbers, for two doors. Mine is from 1976 (the last year these cars were built), so it has another nickname: the Bicentennial Bimmer.

I drive the car almost every day, and it's very responsive, so it's a blast. But working on it is equally as much fun. I've worked in the nuclear energy industry for over forty years, and it can be complicated. The car is very uncomplicated. The only thing that's electronic is the radio, so working on it is like working on a go-kart.

My only regret about buying a 2002? I didn't do it sooner.

# A Bedazzled Mercedes Becomes a Tribute to Prince

### Rebecca Bass, sixty-two, an art teacher at Heights High School in Houston, TX

**THIS PAST WEEKEND** [A.J.: this article originally ran in the Wall Street Journal on April 11, 2017], many thousands turned out for the thirtieth annual Houston Art Car Parade—billed as the biggest such parade in the world. For the past twenty-eight years, I have worked with students to produce a car for the event. This year, our car—called Purple Reign, a tribute to Prince—won the Mayor's Cup, the top honor.

To start out, I buy the car myself with a budget of $500. This year, I bought a late 1980s Mercedes-Benz. I had a group of eight kids, ages fourteen to seventeen, and we started in January. The kids worked every day after school until dark, on weekends, and all through spring break.

On top of the car, they built a replica of Prince's Honda motorcycle from the movie *Purple Rain*. (I teach the kids

*Photography by Julie Soefer*

to weld.) They created sculptures of Prince, his drummer Sheila E., and his longtime bass player, out of foam, stucco, marine varnish, and glitter.

I'm good at begging for things for my students. At a local Corvette place, I got the back end of a 1991 Corvette. We zip-tied the Corvette piece onto the back of the Mercedes and painted it red, for the Prince song "Little Red Corvette." A local jewelry store called Charming Charlie gives us all its broken jewelry and we used it to bedazzle the car.

The parade itself is unbelievable. The kids have been working so hard, and now they are put on a stage. They are competing with artists from all over. They realize that their world is so much bigger than their block and their school. Their self-esteem skyrockets.

It's amazing for me, too. I see my old students who have worked on these cars in the past. They're twenty years old now, or thirty years old, and they come out to give me hugs and see the new car. The experience is priceless.

After the parades, our cars end up in museums and collections, all over the country, even in Europe. This new one I hope ends up in Paisley Park (Prince's estate in Minnesota), which has been turned into a museum. We give these cars to places where they will be seen, and where they will be cherished.

SPECS

The Anderson Family's 1964 Chevrolet C10 pickup

Engine: 292 cu in, inline 6-cylinder

Top Speed: About 65 mph

Tires: Centennial

This 1964 Chevrolet C10 pickup has been in the Anderson family since the 1970s.
ABOVE Daniel Anderson, at the wheel, on the family's ranch in Tom Miner Basin, Montana.

# How a 1964 Chevrolet C10 Became Part of the Family

**Hannibal Anderson, a school administrator living in Mountain Village, AK, and his son Daniel, a contractor from Bozeman, MT**

**HANNIBAL ANDERSON:** In the mid-1970s, my father needed a truck for utility work on the family ranch in Tom Miner Basin in Montana and for another ranch he had in the Mojave Desert in California. My early memories of the truck are of driving it back and forth between the ranches and of the work we had to do: hauling firewood, and pulling horses in a trailer to and from cattle work. The truck had a 292 straight-six engine with pretty good torque, a really good engine for the kind of work we needed to do.

Over the years the family grew a special affection for the truck. Our family never viewed objects as things that you use and discard. The truck became meaningful in terms of our interaction with our work and our landscape. It was like a horse. The relationship went beyond the mechanical experience. I bought the truck from my father around 1980, for somewhere around $500.

**DANIEL ANDERSON:** My father bought "Old Blue" from his father right around the time I was born. Growing up on our ranch in Montana, my siblings, my cousins, we would all get in the truck and pretend to drive it. Sometimes it would die and it would be left in a field for a couple years, then someone would get inspired to get it running again.

When I got my driver's license, the truck was one of the first vehicles I drove. Both my parents, my uncles, my brother-in-law, siblings, ranch workers, all of us have driven the truck at different points in time, and we have all come to associate this truck with our family ranch.

This past summer the truck came into a whole new chapter of its life. We got it running once again, and we used it for work and fishing trips. A filmmaker shot a short fly-fishing film here in Tom Miner Basin and Old Blue got some camera time, so it is getting kind of famous.

It symbolizes struggle, resilience, grace, and rebirth. To us as a family, that means a heck of a lot.

## It symbolizes struggle, resilience, grace and rebirth. To us as a family, that means a heck of a lot.

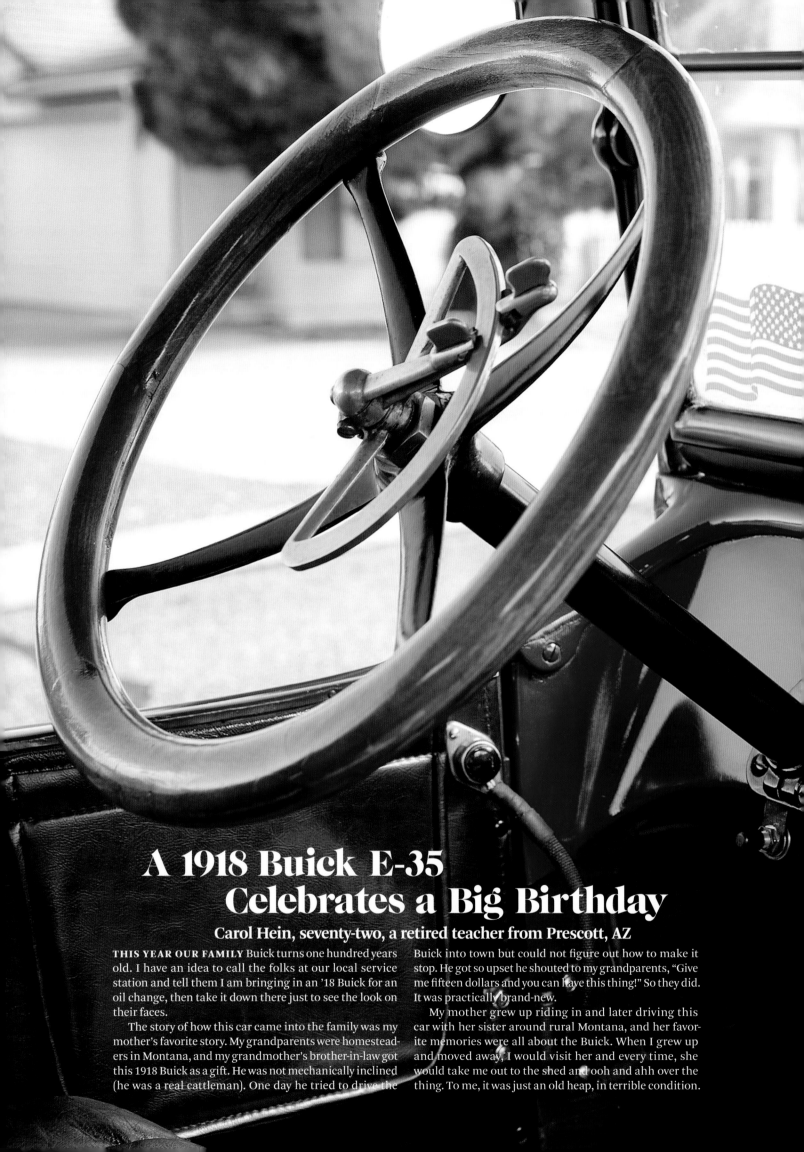

# A 1918 Buick E-35
# Celebrates a Big Birthday

### Carol Hein, seventy-two, a retired teacher from Prescott, AZ

**THIS YEAR OUR FAMILY** Buick turns one hundred years old. I have an idea to call the folks at our local service station and tell them I am bringing in an '18 Buick for an oil change, then take it down there just to see the look on their faces.

The story of how this car came into the family was my mother's favorite story. My grandparents were homesteaders in Montana, and my grandmother's brother-in-law got this 1918 Buick as a gift. He was not mechanically inclined (he was a real cattleman). One day he tried to drive the

Buick into town but could not figure out how to make it stop. He got so upset he shouted to my grandparents, "Give me fifteen dollars and you can have this thing!" So they did. It was practically brand-new.

My mother grew up riding in and later driving this car with her sister around rural Montana, and her favorite memories were all about the Buick. When I grew up and moved away, I would visit her and every time, she would take me out to the shed and ooh and ahh over the thing. To me, it was just an old heap, in terrible condition.

## SPECS

Carol Hein's 1918 Buick E-35

Engine: Inline 4-cylinder

Top Speed: 50 mph

Tires: Universal

There was nothing attractive about it.

When my parents retired, they dedicated themselves to restoring the 1918 Buick. They had to go back to the old homestead to find some of the parts; the backseat they found in a field overgrown with wild rose bushes.

Every year, my husband, two kids, and I would visit Montana in the summer and every year the car would look a little better. My father was excited but my mother—she was ecstatic to see this car that had been such a part of her childhood come back to life.

My parents passed away and the car came into my possession, in 2003. My husband, Scott, is a pilot and he usually drives it. I get nervous. If I screw up, where will I find the parts to fix it? When we are in it, I feel the presence of my grandparents and my parents. It truly is the family vehicle.

Every year we drive the car in our town's July Fourth parade, wearing period clothes. Since this year marks the Buick's hundredth birthday, the parade will be extra special.

# I have an idea to call the folks at our local service station and tell them I am bringing in an '18 Buick for an oil change.

ABOVE Carol and Scott Hein in period clothes with their 1918 Buick E-35. The 101-year-old car has been in her family for three generations.
TOP LEFT The original engine.

Retired champion automobile racer Tommy Kendall stands
atop his "El Gallo" chicken 1973 Oldsmobile Ninety Eight.
Mr. Kendall bought this car some twenty years ago for $895.

## Dream Machines
**Motor racing legend Tommy Kendall's fantasy garage**

| | |
|---|---|
| 1. 1996 All Sport Mustang Trans Am Championship car | 6. Porsche 962 |
| 2. Dan Gurney's Spa GP-winning Eagle Formula 1 | 7. McLaren F1 |
| 3. Porsche 919 Evo | 8. Singer Porsche 911 DLS |
| 4. Porsche 917K | 9. Mercedes-Benz 300 SL Roadster |
| 5. Ferrari 250 TR | 10. 1973 Olds Ninety Eight "El Gallo" |

# The 1973 "El Gallo" Oldsmobile Ninety Eight That Turned into a Chicken

### Tommy Kendall, fifty-one, a retired champion auto racer in the Motorsports Hall of Fame of America and a current television broadcaster, based in Santa Monica, CA

**I AM FORTUNATE** enough to own some rare and expensive race cars, but I would sell any of them before I sold my rooster car.

I heard this vehicle before I ever saw it. I was in my office in Glendale, Arizona, in 1997, when I noticed this noise. I looked out the window, and there was this car with no one in it, clucking like a chicken through a loudspeaker.

A woman appeared, and I offered her $3,500. She drove off, but not before I took some pictures of the car. One of those photos ran in the back of a popular car magazine. Someone called and said the car was in an impound lot and was going to be auctioned off on the following Tuesday. On Monday, I got out $10,000 cash, and the next day, I bought the car for $895.

That was the start of the serendipity with this car that has gone on for twenty years. The stuff that happens, the people you meet, the doors that open, the situations you find yourself in—it's a magic machine.

I named the car "El Gallo"—the Rooster. Since it will not fit in any garage, I have parked it on the street for twenty years.

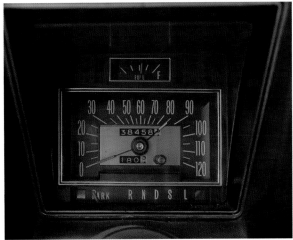

# The car is an unbelievable attitude adjuster. Whenever you get in it, after 10 minutes of people honking, cheering and laughing, you're in a good mood.

Wherever I have lived, the car has lived too, and for some, it has become a Santa Monica landmark.

I once drove El Gallo with my brother across country to Alabama and around the track at Talladega Superspeedway, in front of thousands of fans. The car was once stalked by a famous actress, who would show up in front of my driveway with her daughter to see it every morning. Even animals recognize the car. You pass a guy walking a dog, and the dog goes nuts.

Which leads me to the existential mystery about El Gallo: Why is this 1973 Oldsmobile outfitted like a rooster with a clucking loudspeaker? I do not know. Originally it was owned by a promoter of some kind, in Ohio. I guess it does not really matter.

The car is an unbelievable attitude adjuster. Whenever you get in it, after ten minutes of people honking, cheering and laughing, you're in a good mood. It has attitude, as cocky as they come.

**Who turned this 1973 Oldsmobile into a clucking chicken car? The owner Tommy Kendall is not quite sure, nor does he care. The car is "as cocky as they come," he jokes.**

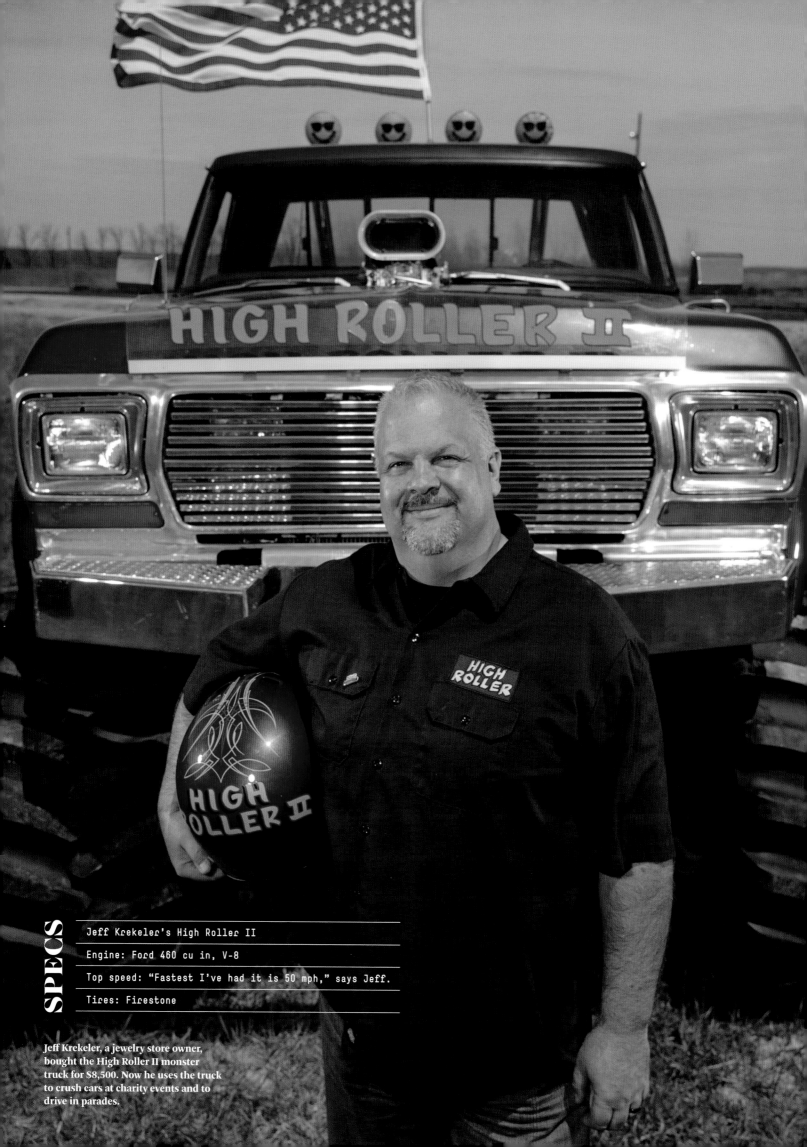

## SPECS

Jeff Krekeler's High Roller II

Engine: Ford 460 cu in, V-8

Top speed: "Fastest I've had it is 50 mph," says Jeff.

Tires: Firestone

Jeff Krekeler, a jewelry store owner, bought the High Roller II monster truck for $8,500. Now he uses the truck to crush cars at charity events and to drive in parades.

# A Monster Truck's Car-Crushing Comeback

**Jeff Krekeler, fifty-two, owner of Krekeler Jewelers in Farmington, MO, and High Roller II**

THE FIRST MONSTER TRUCK, Bigfoot, came out of St. Louis in the 1970s. I grew up an hour south in Farmington, and I remember getting to see Bigfoot's creator Bob Chandler thrash that truck through a mud pit like a mad man, before the truck became a national phenomenon.

A lot of people of my generation remember that truck. For us, Bigfoot was a local hero.

In Farmington, we have a tradition where people turn up for a homecoming parade each fall. For my thirtieth high school reunion in 2014, I had this idea to get Bigfoot to pull a hay wagon in the parade. I shot off an email and, amazingly, one of the truck's early drivers, Jim Kramer, brought the original monster truck to the event.

It was a huge thing for our town. Ever since, people have associated me with monster trucks.

A couple months later, I came in to work one morning and checked Facebook. Six different people had posted a link to a Craigslist ad; the monster truck High Roller II was on sale in Oklahoma. High Roller II was one of the original wave of monster trucks, built in 1985 out of a 1979 Ford F-350, in Fordsville, Kentucky.

The truck had been sitting in a field for years and was in rough shape. I negotiated a price of $8,500, and immediately sold the wheels and tires, so I was only in for about $1,500. I thought it would be fun to have around. I had no plans to restore it. But this is when, for me at least, this story gets really interesting. I am a jewelry-store owner, not a mechanic. But people came out of the woodwork in the monster-truck community to help give High Roller II a new life.

We began to restore the truck inside and out, top to bottom. We re-created all the parts that were missing or broken. One guy helped rebuild a 1980s Pioneer cassette deck.

Now we use the truck in parades and to crush cars for charity events. When you're dealing with a monster truck, everything is amplified—cost and maintenance. Lucky for me, I have a small army of volunteers that helps me keep it going.

> ## I am a jewelry-store owner, not a mechanic. But people came out of the woodwork in the monster-truck community to help give High Roller II a new life.

*Photography by Whitney Curtis*

# A 1954 Lincoln Capri's Italian Pilgrimage

### Jeff Lotman, fifty-six, CEO of Global Icons, a brand-licensing agency, based in Los Angeles, CA

THE MILLE MIGLIA STARTED OUT in 1927 as an Italian race from Brescia to Rome and back—a thousand miles of flat-out speed. In 1957, a famous driver named Alfonso de Portago lost control of his Ferrari, and an accident left about a dozen people dead. The race was canceled. But in the late 1970s, organizers brought the Mille Miglia back as a controlled rally for vintage cars—vehicles that had competed in the original race, or a period-correct make and model of one.

I read about this rally, and along with my old college roommate Brian Grozier—who has since passed away—we began to hunt for a car. I was not keen on spending hundreds of thousands—or even millions—on a vintage Ferrari, Maserati, or Alfa Romeo, but I learned that there were a few American cars that competed in the original Mille Miglia. So I bought a 1954 Lincoln Capri seven years ago, for just over $30,000. This was a car we could actually fit in. (Both Brian and I were over 6 feet.)

In May 2017, the Lincoln finished its fifth Mille Miglia. Compared to the other cars, it's ginormous, and one of the cheapest. The toolboxes of some of these vintage Ferraris cost more than my car. The Lincoln is also very comfortable. It has bucket seats, power windows, an automatic transmission, and a big V-8 engine. At times, you're moving at ninety miles per hour, and it's like driving a sofa.

The event itself is astonishing—four days motoring through Italy. In Siena, we took the car down centuries-old thoroughfares normally closed to vehicles, with stone walls less than a thumb-width on either side of the car. In Rome, the rain came in sheets. In one village after another, you see old couples dressed to the nines sitting at tables with bottles of wine, watching these glamorous cars go by. The event is often called "the greatest antique car rally in the world," and I would agree.

I have had plenty of mechanical problems through these rallies. Before my friend Brian passed away, he nicknamed the car Regan after the character in The Exorcist, because clearly this vehicle is haunted. But it has never failed to finish a rally, and I am already eyeing next year's drive.

**SPECS**

| | |
|---|---|
| Jeff Lotman's 1954 Lincoln Capri | |
| Engine: 5.2 L, V-8 | |
| Top Speed: About 120 mph | |
| Tires: N/A | |

Jeff Lotman has driven this 1954 Lincoln in five Mille Miglia vintage car rallies in Italy.
The car is so comfortable, it is like "driving a sofa," he says.

The nose of a classic 1972 Datsun 240Z, owned by John Naveira. Notice the license plate bracket. Pierre Z is the name of the shop that restored this car.

# And . . . Action!
**Film bigwig John Naveira picks his top-ten motoring movies**

| | |
|---|---|
| 1. Bullitt (1968) | 6. Talladega Nights: The Ballad of Ricky Bobby (2006) |
| 2. Le Mans (1971) | 7. Drive (2011) |
| 3. Smokey and the Bandit (1977) | 8. Gone in Sixty Seconds (2000) |
| 4. Baby Driver (2017) | 9. Tucker: The Man and His Dream (1988) |
| 5. Mad Max (1979) | 10. Vanishing Point (1971) |

SPECS

John Naveira's 1972 Datsun 240Z

Engine: 2.8 L, inline 6-cylinder (replacing the 2.4)

Top Speed: About 140 mph

Tires: N/A

# A 1972 Datsun 240Z
## Gets a Hollywood Ending

### John Naveira of Burbank, CA, an executive vice-president at Sony Pictures

**AT WORK**, my parking spot is at the bottom of a ninety-four-foot-tall rainbow sculpture in Culver City. The rainbow is a nod to *The Wizard of Oz*, which was filmed on what is now the Sony Pictures lot in the late 1930s. When I park my 240Z there everyone can see it, and the symbolism is obvious. It is like a pot of gold at the end of the rainbow.

It was 2012 when my son came home and told me he saw a Datsun 240Z for sale three blocks away. The Z has always been an important car for me, but I had never owned one. When I was in junior high, a neighbor parked her red Z next to my mother's Chevy Impala, and I fell in love with that car.

My wife once owned a 280Z, and both of her brothers have owned 240Zs.

I took a look at this car in my neighborhood, snapped photos, and got the serial number. I sent the photos and serial number to my brother-in-law, Doug Harrison, who still has his 1972 240Z. He did some research and called me.

"That car came into the country just a month after mine," he said. "You have to buy that car." So I did—for $2,200.

What is the Z? Datsun [A.J.: then a division of Nissan in The U.S.] created the 240Z in 1969. Nothing like it had ever existed. This was an affordable and reliable mass-produced

Japanese sports car to compete against more expensive British sports cars. It was a poor man's Jaguar, with a 2.4-liter engine. The car was so successful that Nissan still builds Zs. Today's is called the 370Z. But to me, nothing rivals the first generation, model years 1970 to 1973. I often hear Z fans say that 1972 is the best year.

A friend tipped me off about a local restoration shop called Pierre Z that Nissan has commissioned to restore old Zs, so I had my car restored by the same people Nissan has used. Pierre Z put a bigger 280ZX engine in, and a five-speed manual transmission instead of the four-speed. This really helps in highway driving.

Now the car drives like a dream. All I have to do is change the oil, and it will run forever. I always keep my passenger window open when driving, because I always get a reaction from someone. It keeps people smiling.

# "That car came into the country just a month after mine," he said. "You have to buy that car." So I did—for $2,200.

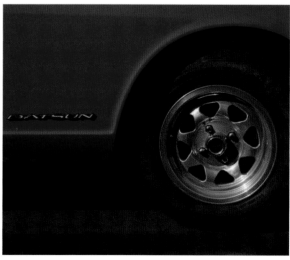

More photos of John Naveira's 1972 Datsun 240Z. Mr. Naveira's parking spot at work
is at the end of a ninety-four-foot-tall rainbow sculpture in Culver City, California.

SPECS

| Josh Siegel's 1955 Chevrolet 210 |
| Engine: 235 cu in, inline 6-cylinder |
| Top Speed: About 85 mph |
| Tires: Goodyear |

Josh Siegel has driven his 1955 Chevrolet 210 in the Woodward Dream Cruise—billed as the world's largest car cruise—over a dozen times. He bought the car for $3,000.

# A 1955 Chevrolet 210 Fit for a Hometown Parade

### Josh Siegel, twenty-nine, a research scientist at the Massachusetts Institute of Technology who lives in Brookline, MA

**THIS SATURDAY**, the Woodward Dream Cruise will roll through Metro Detroit, within a half-mile of the home where I grew up. It is billed as the world's largest car cruise, with over a million spectators. [This column was originally published on August 14, 2018.] I will drive my 1955 Chevrolet 210 in the cruise, for the thirteenth time.

For me the story of this car begins with a summer job, back in 2003. I grew up in Bloomfield Hills, Michigan, a suburb of Detroit that was deep in car culture. When I was fourteen, I taught kids at a summer camp to build model cars. No one in my family worked in the auto industry, but through that summer job I got hooked on cars.

I was just old enough to get my learner's permit (fourteen years, nine months), so I started looking for a vehicle of my own. I found a 1955 Chevrolet 210 in Arkansas, for sale on the internet. I had saved money from my summer camp job and I bought the Chevy for $3,000. Price included delivery, and the car was trucked to a town an hour and a half from our house.

My parents drove me out and I will never forget seeing that car roll off the truck. It was about 11 p.m. and I realized: I did not know how to drive stick. With my father in the car giving me some guidance, I figured it out. It was a terrifying and magical experience.

I did just about everything there was to do on this car. When I disassembled the 235-cubic-inch six-cylinder engine, cleaned it all, and put it back together, it was like going back in time because the car was about three times as old as I was. I studied electronics so I could redo the wiring, and learned about chemistry while stripping paint.

The experience inspired me to study engineering, and today my work involves putting sensors and modems all over vehicles so that you can know everything you need to know about your car through a device, like a phone. When I am tired of work, I escape to the garage in the home where I grew up and my parents still live to work on my 1955 Chevrolet, which has no computers at all.

The Woodward Dream Cruise is something I look forward to all year long. I get to celebrate my Chevy 210 and the car culture where I grew up.

I escape to the garage in the home where I grew up and my parents still live to work on my 1955 Chevrolet.

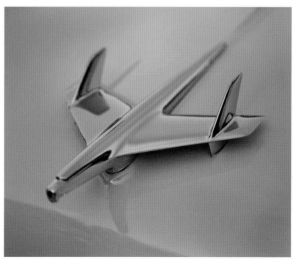

# A 1937 Cadillac Is Poised to Wow Pebble Beach

## Jim Patterson, an entrepreneur from Louisville, KY, and twice winner of the Best of Show award at the Pebble Beach Concours d'Elegance

**THE PEBBLE BEACH CONCOURS D'ELEGANCE** is the most important event in the world for car collectors. Being from Kentucky, I think of it as the Kentucky Derby of car shows. For the last two years, my 1937 Cadillac has been in a constant state of restoration. It is in its final weeks of preparation for Pebble Beach, which is next month. [A.J.: This article originally ran in the Wall Street Journal on July 17, 2018, about five weeks before Pebble Beach.]

The car is one of a kind. Its story begins in Switzerland. In the mid-1930s, a gentleman from Lausanne wanted to buy the biggest, baddest car that could exist in that society. He had the unique idea of special ordering a Cadillac and having it shipped from the U.S. to Lausanne.

In those days, car manufacturers like Cadillac did not always make bodies for their cars. They would supply the frame and motor, and the customer would order a custom body from a body builder.

This gentleman had a firm in Switzerland named Hartmann build the body. The end result was a twenty-two-foot-long car, with a sixteen-cylinder engine. That is like having two V-8 engines, in one. The car and its motor are huge.

World War II disrupted everything in Europe, and this car became derelict, basically left to rot for years. It was ultimately brought into the U.S., I believe, in the late 1960s, and it went through some restoration. A private owner kept it in the Blackhawk Museum, in Danville, California, and three years ago, it came up for sale.

When I bought it, it needed a lot of work and I immediately began a full restoration, hiring RM Auto Restoration in Canada. A tremendous amount of research has gone into finding out what this car looked like when it was new. General Motors supplied original factory build sheets, and we found a gentleman who worked at GM who remembered seeing this car when it was first brought to the States decades ago. He has been very helpful.

Privately, I have showed the car to friends in the car business. Their first reaction is always, "Wow, what is it? A Packard? A Duesenberg?" It is not. It's a Cadillac with a Swiss body.

We are nearing the finish line with our restoration. We are all as excited as we could possibly be to debut the car at Pebble Beach next month. [A.J.: Mr. Patterson's Cadillac won an award at Pebble Beach for "Most Elegant Convertible."]

Jim Patterson and his twenty-two-foot-long custom-bodied 1937 Cadillac. The vehicle has a sixteen-cylinder engine and ample amounts of chrome. "The car and its motor are huge," he says.

The end result was a 22-foot-long car, with a 16-cylinder engine. That is like having two V-8 engines, in one.

# A Vegas Wedding with a Hitch

**Victoria Hogan, twenty-nine, owner of Flora Pop, a pop-up wedding company from Las Vegas, NV, and her Mobile Teardrop Chapel**

THE TEARDROP IS SOMETHING I built myself. It's based on Teardrop travel trailers from the 1950s, and originally, I built it to be a flower stand, using plans I found online. I have an MFA in studio art, my grandfather was a carpenter, and I grew up on a farm, so I could pretty much figure it out.

Then one day it hit me: I was in Las Vegas, the wedding capital of the world. What if I cut out the middleman? I could be the officiant, the florist, and the venue. So I became a civil celebrant [A.J.: someone who can legally officiate weddings], and I turned my Teardrop into a mobile chapel.

The Teardrop has everything you need to hold a pop-up wedding. It carries vintage foldout chairs, a small table, small pullout shelves to put vases on, and buckets for Champagne. I pull it with my Jeep Wrangler, so wherever the Jeep can go, the Teardrop can go too.

I do a lot of garage-sale hunting, and I found a neon sign that says "Sure." It fit perfectly on the back of the Teardrop, so I hung it there. It basically says: "Do you want to get married? Sure!" Everything runs off a single battery. And when the magic time happens, the vehicle itself becomes the altar.

I've officiated nearly forty weddings thus far, since 2014. Many have been in the desert around Las Vegas. I can give the couple coordinates in the desert, and we meet there. I've also officiated weddings in downtown Las Vegas, and in Big Sur and Joshua Tree National Park in California. Sometimes it's just the couple and a photographer. Other times there are a small number of family and friends. Because everything is mobile, I usually bring doughnuts instead of cake, so there's no plates or forks.

My first wedding was on August 16, 2014. It happened to fall on the anniversary of Elvis Presley's death, and living in Las Vegas, that made me think that I was doing what I was supposed to be doing.

Victoria Hogan and her mobile wedding chapel, which she built herself and is based on a 1950s Teardrop travel trailer. Ms. Hogan is a civil celebrant, so she can officiate weddings herself.

# It's Not Just the Porsche, It's the Paint Job

## Bruce Turkel, a branding consultant from Miami, FL, and his 1983 Porsche 911 SC Rally Car Tribute

WHEN I WAS A KID, my dad drove air-cooled Porsches. At the end of the day, I would go down to the end of my street so I could hear the sound of that engine when he came home. He did some rally racing in a Porsche, and to this day, I keep a trophy he won on my desk.

When my oldest daughter graduated college, I bought a 2009 Porsche 911. I love it, but it has a water-cooled engine. [A.J.: Porsche switched from air-cooled to water-cooled engines in the 911 in model year 1999.] The sound is not the same. My Porsche mechanic worked for the mechanic my dad used to go to, and earlier this year, he sent me a note with a picture of this 1983 Porsche rally car replica. He asked, "Is this your next toy?"

My immediate thought was that it was too flashy for me. It was owned by a Miami car collector and I decided to take a look. This owner had the car in a big man-cave. When he started the engine, it was the same beautiful song that I remember from the Porsches my dad drove—that air-cooled engine.

This Porsche has been built out by a previous owner as a replica of a Porsche that raced in the Dakar Rally [A.J.: from Paris to Dakar, Senegal] in 1978—rally racing like my dad did when I was a kid, though not in Africa. The paint job is instantly recognizable to any racing fan. Starting in the 1960s, Martini—the Italian vermouth brand—sponsored racing cars that soon became known world-wide for their bright-striped paint scheme. Rally cars, road-racing cars, circuit cars.

This Porsche's air-cooled 3.0-liter engine is original and has been rebuilt. In fact, everything in this car has been rebuilt, and the air-conditioner has been upgraded. You need that where I live.

I took delivery of the car just a few weeks ago. For my first real adventure in it, I left my house at 4 a.m. and drove across the state of Florida through the Everglades. I may have broken the speed limit. As a rally car, it has special lights so you can see everything around you in the dark.

Every time I get in this car, I think of my dad. He was my hero, and he would have loved this air-cooled Porsche.

# I left my house at 4 a.m. and drove across the state of Florida through the Everglades. I may have broken the speed limit.

The paint scheme on Bruce Turkel's air-cooled 1983 Porsche 911 will be instantly recognizable to racing fans.
For years, Martini has sponsored cars featuring these colorful racing stripes.

**SPECS**

| Bruce Turkel's 1983 Porsche 911 SC Rally Car Tribute |
| --- |
| Engine: 3.0 L, boxer 6-cylinder |
| Top Speed: About 140 mph |
| Tires: Dunlop |

B. WALDEGAARD
H. THORSZELIUS

SHELL
DUNLOP
TELETRON
BOSCH
BILSTEIN

# A 1929 Jack Dempsey Chrysler Imperial Roadster: Emblem of the Roaring '20s

## Joe Wortley, seventy-five, a semi-retired entrepreneur and CPA from Boca Raton, FL

**I AM A COLLECTOR** of things that may seem odd to some, but they have meaning to me. I own an Apollo 13 mock-up that was used in the Tom Hanks movie *Apollo 13*, a nineteenth-century pipe organ that is bigger than a car, and a nearly full-scale re-creation of Charles Lindbergh's Spirit of St. Louis airplane. My most noteworthy car is a Chrysler that once belonged to Jack Dempsey, the world heavyweight boxing champion for much of the 1920s.

I bought the car in 2001 from the late Tom Lester, founder of the Lester Tire Co., who was also a master car restorer. After he restored the vehicle in the 1970s, it won a first-place award at a Classic Car Club of America national competition.

Mr. Lester told me that the car had belonged to Mr. Dempsey. A friend of mine who worked at Chrysler confirmed this fact and sent me a photo he said showed the boxer picking up the car at the Chrysler factory. A quick Google search turns up this same photo. (The car was all black at the time.)

People today don't realize how revered the sports stars of the 1920s were. Babe Ruth, the tennis player Bill Tilden, Mr. Dempsey—these people were unbelievably famous.

The vehicle is interesting for other reasons as well. It was built at a time when Chrysler was still run by its founder—Walter Chrysler—and it is a 1929 model, which means it is emblematic of Roaring '20s extravagance, right before the stock market crashed. The Imperial was Chrysler's high-end vehicle, the company's answer to Cadillac and Lincoln.

As was custom with some high-end cars at the time, the car company would build the mechanical vehicle and a "coach builder" would construct the body, which meant that many of these car bodies were hand-built and unique. My car's body was made by a company called Locke, which also made bodies for Rolls-Royce.

The car has its original six-cylinder engine, just over 5.0 liters. I like to drive it around town. It can be hard to steer (there is no power steering) and parking a car like this in Boca Raton can be quite a project. But the car always draws a crowd, just like Jack Dempsey did back in the day.

This 1929 Chrysler, built when Walter Chrysler himself was still alive, once belonged to Jack Dempsey, heavyweight champion of the world through much of the 1920s.

# I bought the car in 2001 from the late Tom Lester, founder of the Lester Tire Co., who was also a master car restorer.

SPECS

| Jerry Gray's 1952 Buick Roadmaster Riviera |
| --- |
| Engine: 455 cu in, V-8 |
| Top Speed: N/A |
| Tires: Coker |

# Abandoned for Decades,
# a Buick Gets a Makeover

**Jerry Gray, seventy-three, a retired floor-installation business owner
and insurance man from Belgrade, MT , and his 1952 Buick Roadmaster Riviera**

**FOR ME, THE BUICK'S STORY** begins with a plane crash. In 1998, I started building a kit airplane, and when I finished in 2002, I flew it to Florida and safely back. But a month later, I crashed while trying to land. My wife Suzy was watching, and she was not happy. The airplane was totaled, and my wife said to me, "You like old cars. Why don't you keep yourself on the ground?"

I found the Buick on eBay, bought it for $1,500, and drove down to Nebraska to pick it up in a U-Haul, in 2008. The Roadmaster was the top-of-the-line Buick in its day, a true luxury postwar car. But this one had been sitting in a field since about 1965.

In my shop, I disassembled the car and rebuilt it with all new parts—new suspension, four-wheel-disc brakes, fuel injection, rack-and-pinion steering, power everything, and a big 455 Buick engine. I sandblasted the body and my wife and I chose two-tone paint—metallic copper on top, desert rose below. There's SiriusXM radio, air conditioning, plus Truespoke fifteen-inch wheels, and Coker white-wall tires.

A wonderful local artist named Brett McGinley airbrushed a portrait of Marilyn Monroe under the hood. (She was nearing the height of her fame when this Buick rolled off the assembly line.)

The build took me four years and cost about the same as a new Corvette Grand Sport would. The goal was to make a cruiser that my wife would want to spend time in, and it worked, because she loves the car as much as I do. We will motor all day long at seventy-five miles per hour, and we get up to twenty-six miles per gallon on the highway, as much as many new cars today. Everywhere we go, we have to add an hour to our travel time, because when we stop, strangers cannot get enough of this car.

This is an exciting time of year for Suzy and me. Every summer, we get in the Buick and head either east or west, putting ten thousand miles on the car. This summer, we're heading west to visit our kids in California—me, my wife, and Marilyn.

**Jerry Gray and his wife Suzy in their 1952 Buick Roadmaster, which he built out himself.
The car has all modern components, from SiriusXM radio to air conditioning and power everything.**

**The airplane was totaled, and my wife said to me, "You like old cars. Why don't you keep yourself on the ground?"**

SPECS

Gracie Hackenberg's 1999 Mazda Miata Racing Car

Engine: 1.8 L, 4-cylinder

Top Speed: 135 mph

Tires: Bridgestone

# A Built-It-Herself 1999 Mazda Miata Racing Car

## Gracie Hackenberg, twenty-two, a recent graduate from Smith College in Northampton, MA

IN OCTOBER 2017, roughly forty teams from all over the country turned out to compete at the Grassroots Motorsports $2017 Challenge at Gainesville Raceway in Florida. The basic rules were, you build a racing car for no more than $2,017, and that includes all the parts except safety equipment. Drivers were to compete in drag racing, autocross (racing one at a time through a course to see who's fastest), and a concours (participants would have three minutes to present their cars and their stories to judges).

I grew up in a car family, and I started helping my grandfather—a NASA engineer—work on his vintage cars when I was seven. I got hooked on racing around the time I got my driver's license at age seventeen. (I admit, I got some speeding tickets.) As an engineering student, I was looking for a motor-sports project I could take on while in college. The Grassroots Motorsports event was perfect because it was accessible in terms of resources, and a really supportive community.

I began building my car the summer before the event while interning for Hale Motorsports, a race shop in Old Saybrook, Connecticut. Randy Hale, my mentor, sold me a gutted Mazda Miata for $600 and taught me how to weld in a roll cage. The Miata is the most popular production vehicle for people who want to build race cars but do not have professional budgets, so it was an ideal start.

At the beginning of the school year, I took the car to campus. Even though the project was independent (I was not being graded), I got help from fellow students; the lab coordinator for the engineering department, Sue Froehlich, was my main adviser.

At the beginning, I had about forty Smith students helping, but the work got so intense over the last eight weeks (on top of school work), there were only three left at the end. While my teammates raised money for the car and travel expenses through a Smith college engineering grant and a GoFundMe page, I focused on the vehicle. Working in a school machine shop, I installed an exhaust system, fabricated custom seat brackets, and installed the race seat, safety harness, and a spoiler. The 1.8-liter motor and the manual transmission were stock 1999 Miata.

My adviser Ms. Froehlich's husband drove the car on a trailer to Florida, and I flew down to compete. The winners got trophies and bragging rights, and I took home seventh place for the whole Smith College team.

**Gracie Hackenberg in her Mazda Miata racing car. She competed in this vehicle in the Grassroots Motorsports $2017 Challenge in Gainesville, Florida, taking seventh place.**

# The 1948 Babe Ruth Lincoln Continental

## Lonnie Shelton, sixty-five, a semiretired maker of gas compressors from Pampa, TX

ON BABE RUTH DAY (April 27) in 1947, Ford Motor Co. gave a car to Babe Ruth to drive around promoting baseball among kids. The car came from the factory in Yankee blue. The Lincoln Continental was an extraordinarily luxurious car for its time. Ruth had retired from baseball in 1935 and, soon after receiving this car, he died from the effects of cancer, in 1948.

I first discovered the car in a museum in Dallas. I was so fascinated that I started doing research. This car was not just a piece of baseball history, but American history, because Babe Ruth's story is as uniquely American and inspiring as any I can imagine. At seven years old, he was on the streets of Baltimore, surely headed for a future in prison. He ended up in St. Mary's reformatory for delinquents, where he started playing baseball. How a kid like that ends up being arguably the greatest ballplayer ever is incredible.

In 2012, the Lincoln came up for sale, and I bought it. It's never been repainted, nor restored. The previous owner furnished documentation that shows that this car is a 1948 model and that Ruth did own it. [A.J.: The *Wall Street Journal* found an article in the *Boston Globe* from April 27, 1947, saying that Ford gave Ruth a Lincoln Continental and that it was a 1947 model.]

The car has a St. Christopher pendant (the patron saint of traveling) attached to the rearview mirror, which I have been told belonged to Babe Ruth. It also has a stain on the front passenger seat. Babe Ruth loved hot dogs. As the story goes, he once ate a dozen of them before a ballgame. I don't know how to validate this, but the stain on the front passenger seat is in the shape of a hot dog. If I was driving this car and I had a hot dog in my hand, I'd set it down right in the spot where the stain is.

I take this Lincoln to car shows, ballgames, all kinds of events, and raise money to help hospitals for kids. It was built for Babe Ruth to use while helping kids, so I figured that's how I should use it too.

## SPECS

| | |
|---|---|
| Lonnie Shelton's 1948 Babe Ruth Lincoln Continental | |
| Engine: | 292 cu in, V-12 |
| Top Speed: | N/A (speedometer goes to 110 mph) |
| Tires: | N/A |

**The previous owner furnished documentation that shows that this car is a 1948 model and that Babe Ruth did own it.**

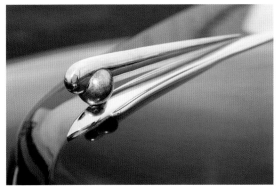

Lonnie Shelton's Lincoln Continental. In 1948, Ford Motor Company gave this car to the baseball star Babe Ruth. A year later, the Babe was dead of cancer, but the car survives.

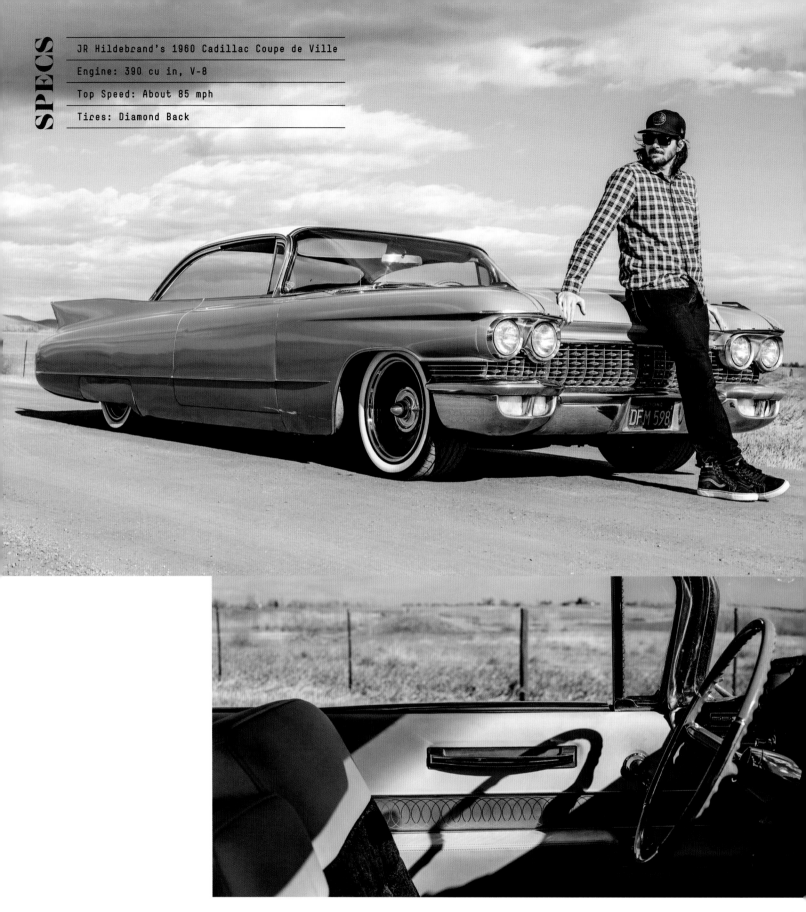

JR Hildebrand's 1960 Cadillac Coupe de Ville

Engine: 390 cu in, V-8

Top Speed: About 85 mph

Tires: Diamond Back

**I thought, wow, there is a lot that could go wrong here. The steering wheel is more of a direction suggester, hardly a precision instrument.**

# How a 1960 Cadillac Coupe de Ville Lets a Racer Slow Down

### JR Hildebrand, twenty-nine, an IndyCar driver and the 2011 Indy 500 Rookie of the Year, from Boulder, CO

**BECAUSE I RACE CARS**, people have this expectation that I am supposed to always drive fast. In reality, I have always loved the idea of having a car that would force me to slow down, to live in the moment in a different way than one does on a racetrack.

In 2012, I started searching Craigslist and eBay. I am a General Motors guy, and I became attached to the idea of getting a giant, old, two-door Cadillac, from the tail end of the Harley Earl era. (Harley Earl is a famed GM designer who retired at the end of the 1950s.) The 1959 is the iconic Cadillac with the giant rocket tail fins. But for me, the 1960 was the one—ever so slightly more understated.

I found Rosie in Palo Alto and negotiated the price down to about $9,500. The owner had named the car because of its color and in a way it felt like picking up a rescue dog. I was not going to change the name. She was a running car but needed work. Over the next few years, I kept the car in California, where I am originally from, and had the interior and the suspension redone. The car had nasty vibration at highway speed, so we spent a lot of time adjusting things.

Last year, I shipped Rosie to my home in Colorado. My fiancée at the time, Kristin, and I were planning our wedding at Devil's Thumb Ranch in Tabernash, Colorado. The car showed up the week before, and there were still kinks to work out. A quarter of the gauges worked, and it had the original 390 V-8 engine.

With my father sitting shotgun, we set out in my first major journey in Rosie, over a huge mountain pass bound for Tabernash. I thought, wow, there is a lot that could go wrong here. The steering wheel is more of a direction suggester, hardly a precision instrument. We made the journey just fine.

Kristin and I are both fans of the nostalgic, so having this beautiful, not-quite-perfect Coupe de Ville as the focalpoint prop of our wedding was such a cool experience. That solidifies why I will never sell this car or change its color. She will always be our Rosie.

**JR Hildebrand and his 1960 Cadillac. The professional racer loves this car because it makes him live in the moment, in a different way than one does on a racetrack.**

## Immaculate Collection
### Champion racer JR Hildebrand's dream garage

| | |
|---|---|
| 1. 1934 Delahaye Type 135 | 6. 1969 Alfa GTA |
| 2. 1934 Bonneville-inspired, chopped Ford Coupe | 7. 1985 Lancia Delta S4 Stradale |
| 3. 1959 Buick Invicta Custom | 8. 1989 Audi RR 20v-swapped VW Doka Syncro |
| 4. 1962 Ferrari 250 GT SWB Berlinetta | 9. 2000 RWD R34 Nissan Skyline GT-R V-Spec II |
| 5. 1965 LS COPO 427/dogbox-swapped Corvette Stingray | 10. 2021 Hackrod La Bandita |

SPECS

| | |
|---|---|
| Bob Boniface's 1962 Ferrari 250 GTE | |
| Engine: | 3.0 L, V-12 |
| Top Speed: | 143 mph |
| Tires: | Pirelli |

This 1962 Ferrari 250 GTE was first purchased by the British actor Peter Sellers, and it made an appearance in one of his films. Today it is owned by Bob Boniface, pictured.

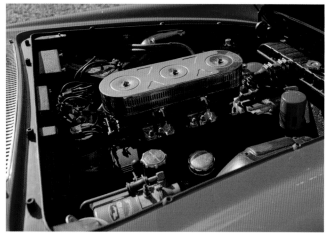

# Enzo Ferrari launched his car company in the late 1940s . . . Our 250 GTE was a window into Enzo Ferrari's work during his heyday.

# The 1962 Ferrari 250 GTE a Family Found Twice

### Bob Boniface, fifty-two, director of exterior design at General Motors' Buick division, from Bloomfield Hills, MI

**MY FATHER, RAYMOND**, was a physician, and when I was growing up, he owned some Ferraris. In 1973, he bought the one pictured here for $3,800 to use as his daily driver. These were not expensive cars at the time.

We knew from the registration card that this Ferrari's original owner had been British actor Peter Sellers. We later learned that the vehicle had been delivered to Mr. Sellers while he was on the set of the 1963 movie *The Wrong Arm of the Law*. The car appears in that movie. (It was white at the time.)

The 250 GTE was the first four-seat Ferrari ever produced in any volume. Enzo Ferrari launched his car company in the late 1940s and he sold a small number of street cars to wealthy clientele to fund his racing program. By the 1960s, he had become the most successful race-car builder in the world. Our 250 GTE was a window into Enzo Ferrari's work during his heyday.

In 1975, my father sold the car for $4,800. He had owned it for two years and made a thousand dollars. He laughed all the way to the bank.

Four years ago, my father found the original owners' manual in his library. It had the registration card with Peter Sellers's signature on it. He called me and said, "You're connected in the car world. You should find that old Ferrari so we can give the owner this manual, as it is an important piece of history."

I looked for the car for three years. Last year, I posted a message on a Ferrari website and I received a private message back saying, "I bought the car from your father over forty years ago and I still have it. I restored it. I am thinking of selling, if you're interested." The guy remembered meeting me when I was a boy.

We struck a deal. It was not cheap, but the owner wanted the car to go to someone who appreciated its history, so he sold it for under market value.

In April 2017, I got the car to my house. My father, now ninety-three, came over. I said, "The last time we were in this car together, you drove. Now it's my turn." We went for a drive. He was over the moon, and so was I.

# A 2000 Ferrari 360 Challenge Built for Nothing but Racing

## Suzy Hiniker, fifty-three, a partner in an IT company outside Boston, MA

THIRTEEN YEARS AGO, I had a eureka moment. Some friends invited me to a track day at New Hampshire Motor Speedway. I showed up in my Maserati street car and got bit by the bug. As much fun as it is to drive a street car on a track, it is way more fun to drive a race car. Some of my friends had Ferrari Challenge cars. Eleven years ago, I bought the one you see pictured here.

A Ferrari Challenge car is a race car created for a racing series called Ferrari Challenge, featured in North America, Europe, and Asia. The race car is based on a Ferrari street car. In 2000, the Challenge car was based on the Ferrari 360, and it was built at the Ferrari factory in Maranello, Italy.

Unlike the street car, this vehicle has no AC, no heat, no electric windows or locks, and no real dashboard. It has an instrument cluster on an LCD display so you can see all the engine data in one place. It also has a roll cage for safety, a fire-suppression system, two race seats, and five-point harnesses in place of the regular seat belts. In essence, it

is lighter and faster than the street car.

It is not street legal, however, so I tow it behind a Ford Excursion to track days. Most are held through the Ferrari Club of America. (I am the director of the New England chapter.) But people show up in all kinds of machinery—Porsches, BMWs, Corvettes, etc. We gather at tracks like Lime Rock in Connecticut, Watkins Glen in upstate New York, or sometimes in the southeast. For longer hauls, I have the Ferrari shipped and I buy a plane ticket.

The car is a cream puff. It makes you look like you are a genius because it is so easy to drive fast. Ferraris are famous for their engine song, and this car's 3.6-liter V-8 has none of the noise-dampening that you find in street-legal cars, so it is especially distinctive.

Part of the fun comes after the driving. At track events, you find people like me who can talk cars all day long. Mostly we talk about lap times. We are all friends, but of course, we all want to be the fastest.

**Suzy Hiniker and her 2000 Ferrari 360 Challenge, a race car that is not street legal. Ms. Hiniker tows this car behind a Ford to track days, mostly in the northeast.**

*Photography by Bob O'Connor*

**SPECS**

| | |
|---|---|
| Suzy Hiniker's 2000 Ferrari 360 Challenge | |
| Engine: 3.6 L, V-8 | |
| Top Speed: 185 mph | |
| Tires: Pirelli | |

**The car is a cream puff. It makes you look like you are a genius because it is so easy to drive fast.**

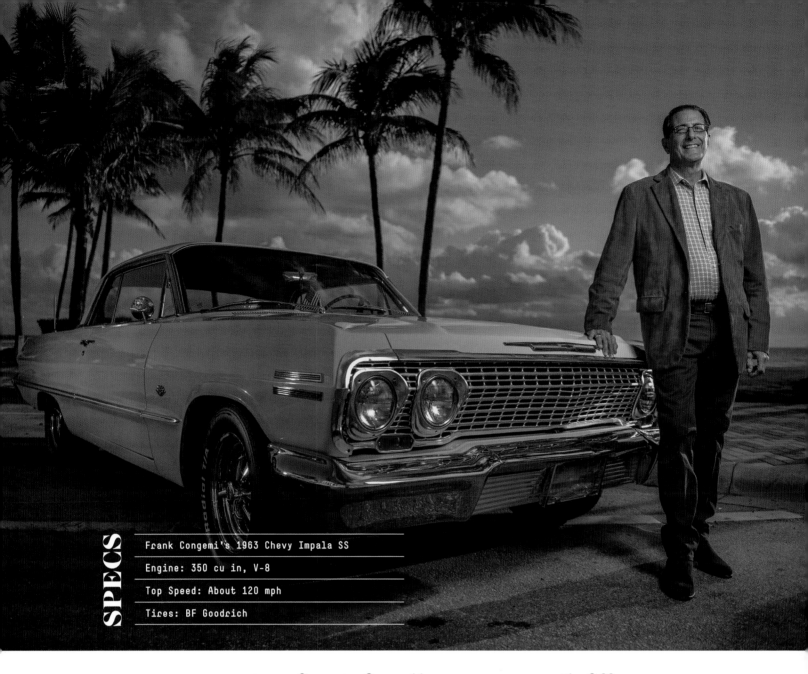

SPECS

Frank Congemi's 1963 Chevy Impala SS

Engine: 350 cu in, V-8

Top Speed: About 120 mph

Tires: BF Goodrich

# Motoring in "Mr. Lucki"

## Frank Congemi, sixty-four, a financial adviser from Deerfield Beach, FL, and Howard Beach, NY, and his 1963 Chevy Impala

**OVER THE YEARS**, I have learned that most men at a certain age come to a realization that they want to buy a car that they have been dreaming about for years. Often it is a car that reminds them of their youth. I am one of those guys, and I come across this all the time helping people figure out their retirements. The car is often part of the dream.

Mr. Lucki started out as a bonding project between my son and me. In 1996, I found a rusty 1963 Chevy Impala SS on someone's yard in Brooklyn and bought it for $1,500. My son and I set out to rebuild the car. Eventually, he got bored and bought a Honda Civic, but I kept on working, because I wanted to set an example. The car became a metaphor for perseverance. The name—Mr. Lucki—is from the Blake Edwards TV show Mr. Lucky, from when I was a kid.

I put a new Corvette engine in the car, disc brakes, Sirius radio, a new automatic transmission, and a new, comfortable interior—everything needed to make this old Impala a modern American cruiser. I travel all over the country visiting clients. Mr. Lucki has been to Maine, Atlanta, St. Louis, New Orleans, and all over Florida.

How do you know if your car is really cool? State troopers pull you over because they want to look at it. I cannot count how many times I have been pulled over. I admit sometimes I am going ninety, but these troopers really just want to see the car. If I can get the officer to talk about his retirement plans, he's not likely to write a ticket.

In the end, I put about $25,000 into Mr. Lucki. To me, the car does not have monetary value, because I will never sell it. I also bought another fixer-upper—a 1969 Dodge Super Bee, which I named Mr. Jimi (after Jimi Hendrix).

These are the kinds of cars I drove when I was in high school. So I guess that means I have never grown up.

**Frank Congemi and his 1963 Chevy Impala SS, which he named Mr. Lucki. Cops pull him over all the time, he says, just so they can take a look at the car.**

# The Spirit of '55 in a Restored DeSoto Fireflite

### Scott McQueen, seventy-one, a retired owner of radio stations from Boca Raton, FL

YOU COULD CALL ME the king of nostalgia. I spent much of my career running oldies radio stations, celebrating the music of my youth. And later in life, I put together a collection of cars that reflect my early years of driving.

When I was in college at Dartmouth, I sold everything I owned to buy a 1965 Corvette. Now I own one of those, in the same color: Nassau blue. In my senior year of college, I bought a 1965 Pontiac Catalina. Now I own one of those. When I first saw some success in radio, I got a 1976 Designer Series Bill Blass Lincoln Continental Mark IV. It was pretty over the top, but that's what I wanted at the time. Now I own one of those.

The most important car to me is the 1955 DeSoto. I got my driver's license in 1963, and the first car I drove was a friend's 1955 DeSoto Fireflite, in red and white, on the streets of Cape Cod, where my family has been summering since I was ten. It was the perfect beach car, and those were life-defining memories.

In the late 1980s, I went looking for a Fireflite, and found one in the exact color scheme in South Dakota. I bought it for $14,000, and I have always kept it at our house in Cape Cod. Every summer, one of the first things I would do when I got up here was figure out how to get that car running.

A few years ago, I realized that this car had become pretty valuable. DeSoto was a division of Chrysler up until model year 1961. The Fireflite was the flagship DeSoto, and a brand-new model for 1955. Only 775 convertibles were made. I asked a friend—Corvette specialist Ronald Garrett of Fort Wayne, Indiana—to restore my DeSoto and its original 291 V-8. He agreed to take on the job, however long it would take. It took three years, and I got the car back this July.

Now it drives like a brand-new 1955 DeSoto. Motoring around this summer, all of my passions came together: the streets and beaches of Cape Cod, the first car I ever drove, and of course, oldies on the radio.

SPECS

Scott McQueen's 1955 DeSoto Fireflite

Engine: 291 cu in, Hemi V-8

Top Speed: About 100 mph

Tires: Coker

# DeSoto was a division of Chrysler up until model year 1961. The Fireflite was the flagship DeSoto, and a brand new model for 1955.

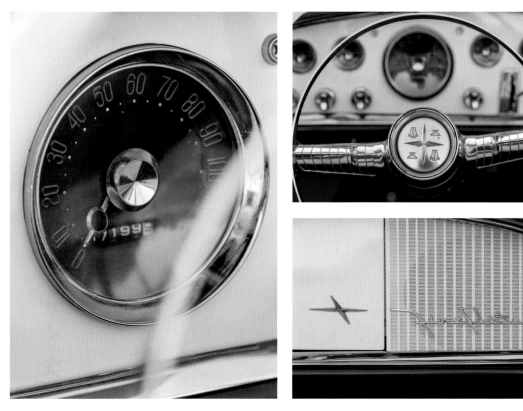

Scott McQueen at the wheel of his 1955 DeSoto Fireflite, in Cape Cod. A career radio man
who owned oldies stations, Mr. McQueen calls himself "the king of nostalgia."

SPECS

Mike Zielinski's 1957 Chevrolet Bel Air

Engine: 376 cu in, V-8

Top Speed: 175 mph

Tires: Nitto

# A '57 Chevy and a Lost Love Memorialized

### Mike Zielinski, fifty-nine, owner of an electrical wholesaling business from Paradise Valley, AZ , and his 1957 Chevy Bel Air / 1959 Airstream Flying Cloud

MY WIFE, TERRI, and I graduated from the same high school class, and in those days, we courted in a 1957 Chevy I owned. I always regretted selling that car, soon after we married. About eighteen years ago, we bought another— same color, same interior. It brought back all those great memories.

In May 2012, my wife died from cancer. When something like that happens, you're left with a huge amount of emptiness. This will sound corny, but I had a vision—a very strong one. When I look back now, I realize this was her way of telling me to move on. I was going to give the 1957 Chevy a full "resto-mod"—make it period perfect on the outside and ultramodern on the inside. At the same time, I was going to buy a period-correct Airstream trailer and do the same. I put a want ad on Craigslist and found the Airstream for about $5,000 just fifteen miles from my house. It's twenty-two feet long.

Friends and family rallied around me. I'd work on the car weekday nights, and the trailer on weekends. Because I worked on both at the same time, I matched them. They share the same upholstery, for example. The project took eighteen months, and I finished last summer.

The car has a 525-horsepower, fuel-injected V-8 engine, custom wheels, independent suspension, disc brakes, air-conditioning, an updated sound system, and a custom-hitch for the trailer. The Airstream, meanwhile, has side and backup video cameras, cork flooring, LED lighting, a refrigerator, microwave, even a new bathtub with beaded curtains. There's a skylight with a piece of leaded glass that my wife made, and I keep a pink bracelet around the car's gear-shifter as a tribute to her.

People ask me: Do you actually use the vehicles? I do. I've pulled that trailer all over the Southwest.

In 2014, I took the 1957 Chevy to my fortieth high-school reunion, and I saw so many old friends who remembered the car I drove back in the day, when I was first dating Terri. She was honored at the reunion. Those kinds of memories, I'll cherish forever.

# I put a want ad on Craigslist and found the Airstream for about $5,000 just 15 miles from my house. It's 22 feet long.

Mike Zielinski's resto-mod 1957 Chevy and the Airstream trailer he fixed up, which has everything from back-up cameras to a new bathtub with beaded curtains.

# A Historic Hot Rod
# Still Ready to Cruise

### Twanna Rogers, seventy-five, co-owner of the Thermal Club, from Palos Verdes Estates, CA and her 1932 Ford Three-Window Coupe Hot Rod

When I was growing up, I remember seeing hot rods in movies. I loved those cars. I was the oldest of eight kids and my mother did not drive. My father needed help driving, so by thirteen, I was already driving our Pontiac station wagon.

Last year, I was at a party at the house of a man who had a collection of cars. There were Porsches and Ferraris, and in the corner of his garage, under a spotlight, he had this 1932 Ford hot rod. I must have circled the car for an hour. I swear it was talking to me. It said, "Twanna, take me home."

I asked the owner if he would sell it and it took three days for him to get back to me. As soon as he said yes, the money was in his bank account.

What is a hot rod? People have debated that question for years, but basically, it is a car built out for speed. And it has to be loud. Decades ago, the 1932 Ford like mine became a favorite car for hot-rodders. [A.J.: The Beach Boys famously

eulogized the 1932 Ford hot rod with their song "Little Deuce Coupe," the deuce standing for the two in 1932.]

My car has a 350-cubic-inch, high-performance Chevrolet V-8 capable of 385 horsepower and a five-speed manual transmission. It is not the easiest car to drive, as there is no power steering. But it is very comfortable. The interior is built so it feels like new Mercedes–quality. When you get in, you feel like you're wearing this car. It is classy, but it does have attitude, the way it rumbles.

At the Thermal Club, a motor racing club that I co-own with my husband, Tim Rogers, there are all kinds of fast cars. But this one stands out. It is not a track car. It is for cruising. I often have my Labradoodle, Jasper, in it with me.

When I pull up, people turn their heads. I get thumbs up everywhere. People are surprised to see a woman driving this car. I can see it in their faces.

My husband and I have many cars. But this one, for me, is extra special. I call it Twanna's Baby.

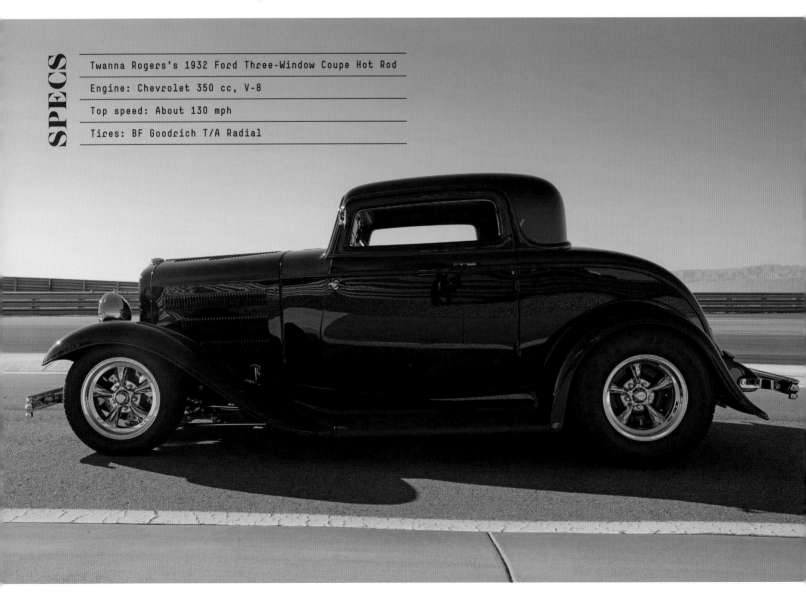

**SPECS**

Twanna Rogers's 1932 Ford Three-Window Coupe Hot Rod

Engine: Chevrolet 350 cc, V-8

Top speed: About 130 mph

Tires: BF Goodrich T/A Radial

# What is a hot rod?
## People have debated that question for years, but basically it's a car built out for speed.

Twanna Rogers at the Thermal Club, in which she is part owner, with her hot rod.
She calls it "Twanna's Baby." "When you get in, you feel like you're wearig this car," she says.

**SPECS**

Doug Manowitz's Homemade Electric Jeep

Engine: 96 V AC motor built by High Performance Electric Vehicle Systems

Top speed: 110 mph

Tires: Goodyear

## The roll bar came from a Porsche Boxster. The electric motor I bought new from a company in California.

# A Homemade Electric Jeep— From the Ground Up

## Doug Manowitz, fifty-nine, a contractor from New York City

**I STARTED THIS** vehicle as a science experiment. I thought, what if I could build an electric vehicle mostly out of parts I could buy on eBay? Essentially out of junk, with some new components added in? It would put out zero emissions, and would cost me nothing to drive. I could plug it in with a regular extension cord wherever I went.

I started with two donor cars that I used to build a chassis: a 1957 VW Beetle and a 1970 Beetle. Then I found a fiberglass replica of a Jeep CJ5 body. All this I brought to a garage in Manhattan where some helpful guys gave me workspace, and I continued collecting components.

When I got to the point that the vehicle would roll, I towed it to the basement garage of my building on the Upper East Side. There, the work continued. I found seats, windshield wipers, rearview mirrors. I tried to keep some sense of color scheme, so the vehicle would be aesthetically pleasing. The roll bar came from a Porsche Boxster. The electric motor I bought new from a company in California. For power, I used eight twelve-volt gel cell batteries, strung in a series, with one extra twelve-volt battery for the light signals, radio, and windshield wipers.

The vehicle took a year to build, and in February 2015, it passed inspection. Collectively, I spent about $15,000. The range is probably twenty miles, but I usually drive no more than five or ten—which is all I need in Manhattan, anyway. I carry a fifty-foot extension cord, and I plan my trips around where I can plug in. At coffee shops, people plug in their laptops. I plug in my vehicle, and I run the wire out the door with a couple traffic cones on the sidewalk so no one trips.

Technically the vehicle sits on a 1970 VW chassis, so it's registered as an old car, and only costs about $300 a year to insure.

In the future, I'd love to start a shop class for high school students. I'd say: Hey, here's this car I built. It's useful, and a lot of the materials are recycled. You can build one, too. That would be a win-win.

**Contractor Doug Manowitz built this electric vehicle entirely himself.
At coffee shops, he plugs the car in and runs the cord through the front door.**

SPECS

The Killorin Family's 1923 Duesenberg Model A

Engine: 260 cu in, inline 8-cylinder

Top speed: 80 mph

Tires: N/A

# A Duesenberg That's a Family Tradition

**Andy Killorin, twenty-three, of Weybridge, VT, and his 1923 Duesenberg Model A**

**WHEN MY GRANDFATHER** Karl was about my age, he spent a year working at the Duesenberg factory in Indianapolis, from 1929 to 1930. He saved his factory uniform. In 1948, he bought the foundation of a Duesenberg Model A, and began to restore it.

It was a long process, and my dad helped him. My grandfather got most of the way before he died in 1988. About ten years ago my dad said to me, "Let's finish this." We completed it in the summer of 2010—sixty-two years after my grandfather started the job. If you look at all the subtleties of a 1923 Duesenberg, they're all correct on the car.

We took it to a car show in Michigan. I'm the same body type as my grandfather. (I was even named after him; my middle name is Karl.) His uniform fits me like a glove, so I wore it to the show. Nobody had worn it since he took it off in 1930. Others were wearing blazers and ties, but I had this uniform on, covered in decades-old oil stains. People went crazy. And the car won two awards.

Now, when I'm wearing the uniform and driving the car, it's the ultimate feeling, like my grandfather is up there looking down on me.

# When I'm wearing the uniform and driving the car, it's the ultimate feeling, like my grandfather is up there looking down on me.

# Big Love for a Tiny 1955 Messerschmitt KR175

### Ralph Hough, seventy-four, the deputy mayor of Oro-Medonte, Ontario

THE WEEK BEFORE I married my wife Wendy in 1962, we bought our first microcar, a Messerschmitt. We lived in England at the time and we went on our honeymoon in this car. Later we toured Europe in it, and in 1964 visited the Messerschmitt factory in Regensburg, Germany, right around the time the company stopped producing these vehicles.

Back then, microcars were called bubble cars, and they were quite popular, most notably the Messerschmitt (like ours) and the BMW Isetta. These vehicles first appeared in the early 1950s, not long after World War II, when resources like steel and fuel were scarce. (Messerschmitt built fleets of German military planes during the war.) Bubble cars made sense. They were efficient, did not use a lot of raw materials, and unlike scooters, protected riders from the weather.

Today, we have six Messerschmitts and one BMW Isetta, and we host a festival on our property called Micro North every June. We get forty to fifty oddball cars from all over the northern States and Canada.

This year's party was extra special because it was the twenty-fifth year. It also marked the fifty-fifth year since my wife and I bought our first microcar, and our fifty-fifth wedding anniversary. We collect these cars because of the sentimentality, because we had such memorable adventures in them when we were young.

The red car you see pictured here is a three-wheeled 1955 Messerschmitt KR175. It has a 175-cubic-centimeter motor that is bolted right to the car's frame with no rubber engine mounts, so the vehicle is a real boneshaker. It is kind of a hybrid between a car and a scooter, in that it has handlebars and a motorcycle-style gear shifter, plus carlike foot pedals. It cruises comfortably at about fifty miles per hour. At a constant speed of thirty miles per hour, it could probably get close to one hundred miles per gallon.

I bought this Messerschmitt from an owner in Montreal approximately twenty years ago, and it was a real basket case. I used parts from five other Messerschmitts in the restoration. I have no idea how much the vehicle cost because I have purposely avoided adding up the bills.

My wife and I have had wonderful adventures in microcars with other microcar fans. We like to do our part to keep these vehicles on the road so future generations can enjoy them too.

## Bubble cars made sense. They were efficient, did not use a lot of raw materials, and unlike scooters, protected riders from the weather.

**SPECS**

Ralph Hough's 1955 Messerschmitt KR175

Engine: 175 cc, single-cylinder

Top Speed: Around 60 mph

Tires: Carlisle

*Photography by Jennifer Roberts*

# A 1938 Indian Sport Scout: Motorcycle History on the Jersey Shore

## Brittney Olsen, 27, a mom and a vintage motorcycle racer from Aberdeen, SD

**WHEN I WAS THREE**, my dad showed me the movie *Heart Like a Wheel*, about the female drag racer Shirley Muldowney. Then, he took me to a drag race in Nebraska and introduced me to her. From that time on, I've always wanted to be a racer. I raced four wheelers, and at fourteen, I started drag racing a 1969 Camaro my dad rebuilt. But eventually, I fell in love with antique motorcycles—Excelsior boardtrackers, Wall of Death Indians and Harley-Davidson Panheads and Knuckleheads.

In 2011, I met Matt Olsen. He wanted me to do some pinstriping on a motorcycle he was building. We hit it off, and when he asked me to marry him, he said he couldn't afford a ring. He asked if he could give me a 1923 Harley-Davidson motor instead. I always knew someday I would meet the perfect man for me. In 2012, we married and, a year later, we started 20th Century Racing. We travel around the country racing old bikes and raising awareness about the history of motorcycle racing in America. Right now, in our garage, we have a few Harley-Davidsons from the 1930s through the 1950s.

SPECS

Brittney Olsen's 1938 Indian Sport Scout

Engine: 45 cu in

Top speed: 85 mph on banked asphalt oval speedway

Tires: Avon

The pictures here were taken at an event called The Race of Gentlemen, in Wildwood, New Jersey, in early June. It's like an amazing time hop. You see the boardwalk, and you're like, hey, I'm in the 1950s. Then you see the old cars and motorcycles and the ocean—there's nothing more antique than the ocean.

The bike is a 1938 Indian Sport Scout I named The Spirit of Sturgis, a tribute bike to the Sturgis Motorcycle Rally, the largest motorcycle rally in the world, which takes place annually in my home state. It's a purpose-built race bike, with the original frame and the original 45-cubic-inch motor. The gas tank and the handlebars are custom made.

Before this race, I got goosebumps thinking of all the people back in the day who raced their bikes and cars on this beach. But once the flag dropped, I wasn't thinking about that. I was thinking about speed.

## He asked if he could give me a 1923 Harley-Davidson motor instead. I always knew someday I would meet the perfect man for me.

**Brittney Olsen racing her 1938 Indian Sport Scout. Ms. Olsen was first inspired to race by the drag racer Shirley Muldowney, whom she saw in the 1983 film *Heart Like a Wheel*.**

# A Honda CRF450R with a Bite

## Shayna Texter, twenty-six, a professional motorcycle racer from Willow Street, PA

FLAT-TRACK MOTORCYCLE racing is probably the oldest form of motorcycle racing in America. We race on dirt ovals all over the country. I am one of only two women competing in the American Flat Track single-cylinder series and I am leading the points championship. No female has ever won this championship, and I'm hoping to change that this year.

My father raced professionally and he owned a Harley-Davidson dealership, so he had me riding a motorcycle at three years old. My brother Cory (also a pro racer) and I were given a choice when we were growing up: help my dad work on bikes or go to the gym. I always loved working on motorcycles, and it is still my favorite hobby when I am not racing.

The bike I am riding now is a showroom 450-cubic-centimeter single-cylinder Honda motocross bike that we converted to a competition bike. [A.J.: Ms. Texter is sponsored by a Dallas Honda dealership.] We put racing suspension and nineteen-inch wheels on, so the bike sits a lot lower than a stock bike. We also took off the front brake.

On the track, riders wear full leather suits, leather gloves, a full-face helmet, and boots, plus a steel shoe that attaches to the left boot, as we use the left leg to slide through turns when we are turning left.

The bike can hit 130 miles per hour, and there are literally times when riders are bouncing off each other, racing handlebar to handlebar and wheel to wheel. This requires a lot of trust in your competitors, because one little bobble and you can be on your way. Unlike a racing car, there is no roll cage. It's literally your body hitting the ground. I have never had any major injuries. I broke my foot a couple times and my shoulder blade once.

When I put my helmet on, I do not think of myself as a female. I am just a motorcycle racer. But when that helmet comes off and I hear the crowds screaming and cheering for me, I get so inspired. Because I feel like I am inspiring other people to push harder and to go after their dreams.

**Shayna Texter with her Honda. Ms. Texter travels the U.S. competing in the American Flat Track series, which she calls "probably the oldest form of motorcycle racing in America."**

*Photography by Angela DeCenzo*

SPECS

Shayna Texter's Honda CRF450R

Engine: 449 cc, single-cylinder

Top Speed: N/A

Tires: Dunlop

# A 1937 BMW R5 and a Tour Through History

## Philip Ernst Richter, forty-five, president of Hollow Brook Wealth Management in New York, NY

**THE 1930S WAS A TERRIBLE** era in so many places around the world, but especially in Germany. To me, BMW motorcycles from that era are like a silver lining. The engineering was out of this world. And the bikes are so beautiful.

My father grew up in Germany during the war. He told stories of riding his motorcycle around Hamburg afterward. When I was six, we lived in Greenwich, Connecticut, and he bought me a Honda 50. That bike kicked off my love of motorcycling; I still have it today.

Right now, I have eleven BMW motorcycles, many of them from the 1960s or prewar. The R5 is the Holy Grail of prewar BMWs. It's unique in that it was a low-production bike built only in 1936 and 1937. It was a technical tour de force, a superbike of its day. It had overhead valves and adjustable front forks.

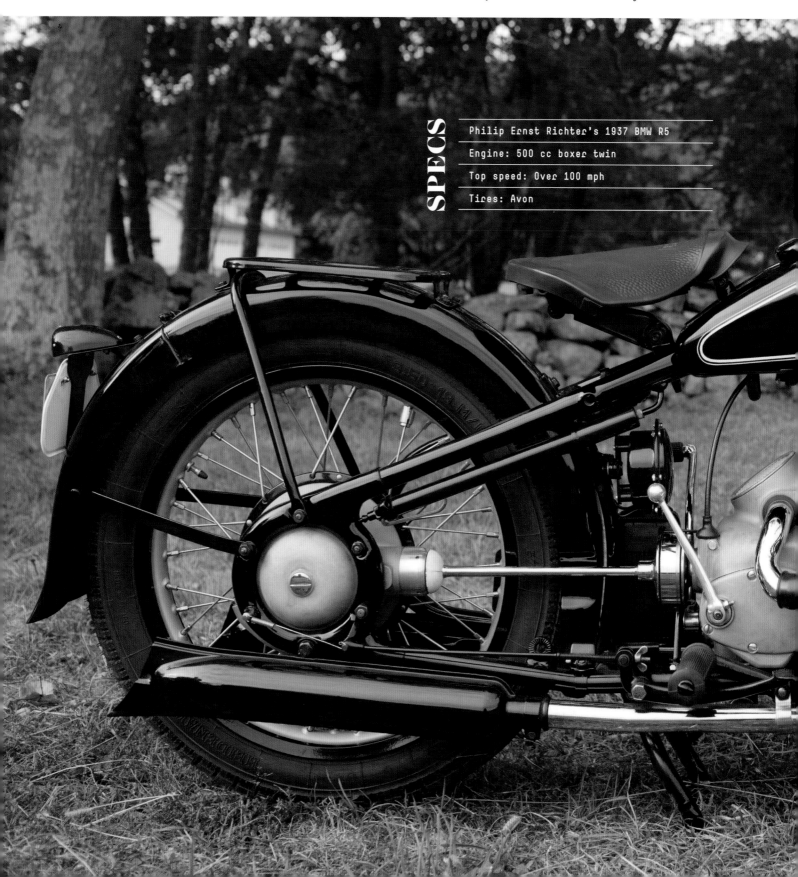

SPECS

Philip Ernst Richter's 1937 BMW R5

Engine: 500 cc boxer twin

Top speed: Over 100 mph

Tires: Avon

Unlike earlier BMWs, this one was fast and powerful, but also comfortable to handle. I could get it on it now and ride across country, at today's speeds.

My R5 was the eighth-last one ever built (coming off the assembly line December 2, 1937), and that's been documented by the historical archives at BMW in Germany. It has certain things that are unusual. For example, the muffler is not chrome, because leading up to wartime, materials like chrome were difficult to obtain. The bike was shipped new to a dealership outside London, and that's the key to its condition today. Most bikes that stayed on the continent were destroyed during the war or picked apart after for parts.

I have a documentation file on this bike a mile long. I know the name of the original owner, and his phone number and address at the time. I have service reports from the original dealership. Most important, I was able to document the authentic serial numbers showing that the frame and the engine are original. That's extremely rare.

To me, these bikes are industrial art. When I ride the R5 today, it makes this incredible sound. It's like a symphony.

SPECS

Elias Kirtz's MZ Silver Star Classic Gespann

Engine: 500 cc, single-cylinder

Top speed: About 70 mph

Tires: N/A

# 1996 MZ Silver Star Classic Gespann: Converting the Dregs to Good Use

## Elias Kirtz, forty-four, a carpenter from Long Island City, Queens, NY

**MY GARAGE SPACE** is full of weird objects. I have the bicycle I used for my fifth-grade paper route, and an engine from a 1966 station wagon. But mostly, I keep my motorcycles in there.

I own the dregs of the motorcycle world, the kind that are completely worthless unless you put a million hours into them. I try to get them for nothing and get them running, and I don't care what they look like—mostly 1960s Hondas, since so many were made. I've been commuting to jobs all over New York for years on bikes with less horsepower than two weed whackers, in rain, snow, or sunshine.

I have six bikes in the garage now. My helmet is a police helmet, and it cost more than several of my motorcycles.

The MZ Silver Star Classic Gespann, however, is an exception. It defies my logic, because it's actually a nice bike. It's an oddity—a big angry machine—but it's also practical. It was built in eastern Germany in 1996. That's after the

Berlin Wall came down, but in the same old factory where MZs were built for years before that. I found it on eBay this past summer and bought it in Latrobe, Pennsylvania. The whole rig fit in the back of my pickup truck.

The bike's got a 500-cubic-centimeter single-cylinder—a thumper, as they call bikes with one big cylinder, because of the sound. Not a lot of these bikes were imported, and MZ has since all but disappeared from the motorcycling world.

A lot of times, sidecars are thrown on bikes haphazardly, but this sidecar was built properly with the motorcycle at the factory. Mostly, my girlfriend rides in the sidecar. But people from the neighborhood are always asking—especially kids, and they're not allowed unless they ask their parents first.

At our block party last summer, I gave rides in the sidecar until the clutch cable broke. I was literally not allowed to stop. Giving all those rides made buying this bike worthwhile.

**Elias Kirtz is into the "dregs of the motorcycle world." The bike pictured here is a MZ Silver Star Classic Gespann, built in eastern Germany in 1996.**

**The bike's got a 500-cc single-cylinder—
a thumper, as they call bikes with one
big cylinder, because of the sound.**

# "Wind Therapy": A Modified 2018 Indian Scout Bobber

### Richard Neider, thirty-nine, a U.S. Army veteran from Phoenix, AZ

I GOT INTO MOTORCYCLES when I was seven. I started on a minibike with a lawn-mower engine, and I kept riding bigger and bigger bikes. In 2005, I was injured while serving in Operation Iraqi Freedom. My injury progressed and in 2011, I stopped riding because I could no longer hold up a bike. In January 2013, I lost my ability to walk. Anywhere I had to go, I had to ask somebody to take me.

In 2017, at the Sturgis Motorcycle Rally in South Dakota, the Veterans Charity Ride [A.J.: a charity that helps wounded veterans with "motorcycle therapy" and other programs] got me on a modified Indian motorcycle with a mentor. I rode in a sidecar. After, I talked with my wife, Kerry, and we started saving some money so we could build our own bike.

On February 23, 2018, I picked up an Indian Scout Bobber. An Arizona dealership called Double D's Performance sold me the bike at cost. Through Veterans Charity Ride, a lot of people started donating parts, and a guy named John Meade at Azzkikr Customs [A.J.: a custom-motorcycle builder and repair shop] near where I live began to build my bike. On July 3, I rode the Indian for the first time.

The handlebars are big and sturdy, so I can wheel up in my chair, pull myself onto the bike with the handlebars, then fold up my chair. There's a wheelchair mount on the back of the sidecar, and special footboards that keep my feet in place. Everything from a parking brake to a modified clutch system is built so that I can operate the bike with my hands alone.

The first time I rode the bike, I had this flood of emotion, what I call "wind therapy." Not only was I able to go to that spot I used to go in my mind that helps me get through everything, I was able to be independent again. I could go where I wanted without asking for help.

I left Arizona with nineteen other riders for a roughly 1,700-mile journey through Colorado and Utah to the Sturgis rally. Last year, a mentor showed me that I could ride again. This year, I will be a mentor, and I will get to show someone else that they too can get back out there.

**SPECS**

Richard Neider's Indian Scout Bobber

Engine: 69 cc, V-Twin

Top Speed: 136 mph

Tires: N/A

This past weekend, I left Arizona with nineteen other riders for a roughly 1,700-mile journey through Colorado and Utah to the Sturgis rally.

Richard Neider on his modified Indian Scout Bobber. Mr. Neider was injured while serving in Operation Iraqi Freedom. This bike is built so he can operate it without the use of his legs.

Jeffrey "Meatloaf" Scales's Custom 2006 Harley-Davidson Street Rod

Engine: 96 cu in, V-Twin

Top Speed: About 130 mph

Tires: Vee Rubber

**Jeffrey "Meatloaf" Scales hits the streets on his custom Harley-Davidson Street Rod.
Mr. Scales built out this Harley himself to express his style and his love of motorcycling.**

# Part Harley-Davidson, Part "Spaceship"

### Jeffrey "Meatloaf" Scales, forty-nine, a heavy-duty tow-truck driver with the New York City Department of Sanitation

**GROWING UP IN BROOKLYN**, I was always into motorcycles. I wanted one so bad, but I could not afford one. I finally saved up enough to buy a Honda CBR1000 when I was twenty-five. Then one day I went to a Greek festival in Philadelphia, and I saw these three guys ride up on Harley-Davidsons. It drove me nuts how bad I wanted one. So I started saving.

In 2003, I got my first Harley. I started modifying it, working in a shop in Brooklyn. I am laid-back but I am really flashy, too. I wanted the bike to be a representation of who I am. I wanted to take the whole idea of what a Harley-Davidson is and turn it upside down, so to speak. So I built something truly different, with a twenty-six-inch front wheel.

Back then, in Brooklyn, nobody was riding Harleys with front wheels that big, and people took notice. The bike ended up on the cover of *IronWorks* magazine.

I decided to build another. And another. The bike you see here is my third. I bought a 2006 Harley-Davidson street rod in 2010, modified the neck to fit a thirty-inch wheel, redid the stereo, added custom body parts, and upgraded the suspension so the ride is extra smooth. The paint is Lamborghini Tiffany Blue. The whole build took nine months.

I left the engine pure Harley-Davidson. On a previous bike, I customized the engine, but in New York there is so much starting and stopping and I found that the engine would overheat. So this time, I left the motor stock.

Now this bike is like a spaceship, and I cruise all over the city. Every year I ride in a charity event called the Distinguished Gentleman's Ride—thousands of motorcycle riders wearing suits cruising in cities all over the world—to benefit cancer research. In the winter I wear fur coats. People see me and think, "This guy's crazy." But people who know me know that I'm just Meatloaf. I got my own style.

I am working on my fourth bike, and my goal is to have my own line of custom Harley-Davidson motorcycles someday. That is my dream, and I am going through the stages to get there.

## Who Needs Leather?
### Jeffrey "Meatloaf" Scales's motorcycling fur coats

1. Chinchilla fur coat, white and gray
2. Beaver, brown and tan
3. Mink, silver
4. Fox, beige

## I decided to build another. And another. The bike you see here is my third.

Tony Cochrane's 1967 Quadrophenia Lambretta

Engine: 150 cc

Top speed: N/A

Tires: N/A

**This scooter, ridden by the film's main character, Jimmy Cooper, becomes a centerpiece of the movie. Jimmy is seen riding it through London constantly.**

# 1967 Quadrophenia Lambretta: The Ultimate Mod Scooter

## Tony Cochrane, an owner of nightclubs, from Dundee, Scotland

**AS A MOVIE MEMORABILIA COLLECTOR,** I have the baseball bat that Robert De Niro's character wields in *The Untouchables* and the box where Al Pacino's character in *Scarface* keeps his illegal goods. When the *Quadrophenia* scooter came up for auction in November 2008, I was in London and I thought I would go have a look.

The 1979 movie *Quadrophenia* is from The Who's rock opera of the same name, which chronicles the period after the Depression and the war in the 1960s, when a youth movement first crystallized on the streets of London. Great R&B music was coming out, and there were these young rebels fighting the establishment and creating their own scene. It was about music, style, and scooter gangs, and they called themselves the Mods. They were influenced by Italian culture—the cool suits and shirts and Italian-made scooters.

This scooter, ridden by the film's main character, Jimmy Cooper, becomes a centerpiece of the movie. Jimmy is seen riding it through London constantly, and his search for excitement and acceptance on this scooter becomes a symbol for the search of a whole generation for an identity. When the movie came out in 1979, the film sparked a revival of Mod culture, which still exists today.

The scooter is a 1967 Lambretta Li150 Series 3, tricked out for the movie with trademark mirrors all over the front. When it went up for sale at the auction in London, I got sucked into the whole thing and I felt that I had to have it. I bought it for £36,000 pounds (about $45,000), and I keep it at my home. It is a museum piece now. I wouldn't want to ride it and risk anything happening to it.

When I bought it, the sale was covered by the press in the U.K., so word went around that I had Jimmy's scooter. People still come knocking on my door—Mods who are on pilgrimages to see the thing, because it is still a Holy Grail of Mod culture today.

# Grandmother's Goal: A Cross-Country Motorcycle Trip at One Hundred

## Gloria Tramontin Struck, ninety, and her 2004 Harley-Davidson Heritage Softail Classic

**I WAS BORN** in a little apartment behind a motorcycle shop in Clifton. My father had started the business in 1915—one hundred years ago. Even as a baby, I was with motorcycles every day of my life. When I was sixteen, my brother decided I should learn to ride. I told him, "I'm not going to do it! And you can't make me." But he convinced me. Now seventy-four years later, I'm still riding.

My first motorcycle was a 1941 Indian Bonneville Scout. Over the years, I've owned three Indians and eleven Harley-Davidsons. Since 1950 I've been riding long distances, to races and events all over the country, and in Europe.

The first time I rode to Daytona Bike Week in Florida, was in 1951. And I still ride to Daytona. The first time I rode from New Jersey to the Sturgis Motorcycle Rally in South Dakota was in 2003. I've gone every year since, and I'm in the Sturgis Motorcycle Museum's Hall of Fame.

This summer, my granddaughter and I rode our Harley-Davidsons to the seventy-fifth Sturgis rally. Before we left, a friend started talking about us on Facebook, saying, "Keep an eye out for Gloria Struck, on her way to Sturgis. She's ninety years old, riding a blue Heritage Softail Classic. Her granddaughter's on a red Sportster."

I'm not exaggerating: Every time we stopped for gas, every time we stopped for something to eat, people were watching for us. One woman came up and said, "Excuse me, is your name Gloria?" I said yes. She turned to her friends and yelled, "Hey, it's her! It's her! It's Gloria!"

We had three days to get to Sturgis—close to 1,800 miles one way. We spent so much time talking to people and taking pictures with them, we had to ride eighty miles per hour to catch up on time. And it happened all over again on the way back.

When I'm one hundred years old, I plan on riding across country on two wheels. I believe it'll be the first time anyone's done it—male or female. I'm very active, and I love new challenges. I always tell people: Live your dreams.

## The first time I rode from New Jersey to the Sturgis Motorcycle Rally in South Dakota was in 2001. I've gone every year since.

At ninety years old, Gloria Tramontin Struck is still riding her Harley-Davidson across the country.
BELOW  A painting of Ms. Struck and one of her bikes, from many years ago.

# 1967 Aermacchi Harley-Davidson: A Bike Rebuilt to Break a Record

### Stacie B. London, an art and design consultant and sales associate/brand ambassador for Double RL (a division of Ralph Lauren), based in Los Angeles, CA

**MY FATHER,** Tony, is a gearhead, and in 1965, he set a land-speed record for a certain class of car at the Bonneville Salt Flats in Utah. I spent a lot of time in his shop, and for me, there was always this idea of a motorcycle in my head.

I bought my first bike in 2009—a 1969 BMW R60US that I still have. A year later, I went to a vintage motorcycle race at Willow Springs International Raceway in California. I had grown up watching Nascar on TV with my dad, but I had never seen real racing in person.

I decided this was something I needed to do, so I bought a 1968 Honda 160 and began road racing in 2011. In 2015, the American Historic Racing Motorcycle Association named me Lady Roadracer of the Year.

It was through road racing that I met my mentor Ralph Hudson, who has taught me so many things about how to modify motorcycles to get the most speed out of them. To give back, I have helped crew for Ralph in land-speed-record racing. Last year, he set a record for

**Stacie B. London and her 1967 Aermacchi Harley-Davidson, which she has used to go land speed record racing on the Bonneville Salt Flats in Utah.**

**SPECS**

| Stacie B. London's 1967 Aermacchi Harley-Davidson |
| Engine: 250 cc, single-cylinder |
| Top speed: 97.993 mph |
| Tires: Avon |

*Photography by David Walter Banks*

# The one that most excited me was an Aermacchi, a rare Italian motorcycle imported by Harley-Davidson beginning in the early 1960s.

a class of motorcycle, at 266.399 mph. This inspired me to attempt to become a second-generation land-speed-record-holder.

I searched the record books and found that the record for the 250-cubic-centimeter push-rod class felt soft—something I could achieve. There is a short list of bikes that fit this category, and the one that most excited me was an Aermacchi, a rare Italian motorcycle imported by Harley-Davidson beginning in the early 1960s.

It turned out a friend in San Francisco owned one and agreed to sell it. I bought it in February 2018 and spent

three months rebuilding it. I made my rookie runs at El Mirage, a dry lake bed in California's Mojave Desert, in May, then raced again in June and July. I took the bike to Bonneville for Speed Week in August. The record for my class is 83.148 mph. At Bonneville, my speed was only 1.333 mph off.

Earlier this month, I loaded the Aermacchi in my 1970 Ford F-100 pickup and headed back to El Mirage to try to break the record. I made two passes, but the record was still out of reach. When the season begins in May, I will try again.

# Acknowledgments

OVER THE COURSE OF NEARLY twenty years writing for newspapers and magazines, I have worked with some wonderful professionals, but none more so than the editors at the *The Wall Street Journal*. The My Ride column has been a true blessing since the first one appeared on August 27, 2013. The column was conceived by Leslie Yazel, formerly of the *The Wall Street Journal*, while Adam Thompson at the *Journal* has guided the column's scope and focus since the start. Thank you, Adam. You are a hawk for nixing clichés, so I'm sorry for this one: You are a true joy to work with. Should that be a true joy with whom to work? I don't know. You're the best.

Thank you also to Leah Latella, the great photo editor who has guided the column from a photo perspective for years and did the photo editing work in the creation of this book collection. Leah is a star and she has brought tremendous creativity and reliability to the My Ride column. No matter where on earth we found a cool story, Leah has been on the case with a local photographer who can shoot the story beautifully.

Thank you to all the photographers whose work appears in this book and whose work has appeared in the My Ride column. In every case, you went above and beyond expectations. I hope this book and the column contributes in some way to your legacy of excellence.

Thank you to Lisa Bannon and Emily Nelson at the *The Wall Street Journal* for having me. More thank yous to Dagmar Aalund, who has edited many of the columns over the past eighteen months. Barbara Scott and Allison Scott (not related) handled photography for the column the first few years of its existence. Other editors include Michael Boone, Larry Greenberg, Barbara Chai, and Missy Sullivan. You all have my absolute appreciation.

After the first couple years of the column's existence, I began to think about how I could create a book collection. But I never thought I would be lucky enough to work with Rizzoli. When describing Rizzoli to friends and colleagues, I usually say it is "the world's most prestigious publisher of art, photo, and coffee table books." Thank you to James O. Muschett for your belief in this project, and for opening Rizzoli's doors to me. Thank you to Elizabeth Smith, who handled all the copy editing on this book. Edward Leida and Sherry Wang handled the design of the book, and, if I may be so bold, it looks dynamite.

I want to thank Mario Andretti—the only athlete I can think of who has been for most of his life on a first-name basis with the entire world—for writing the book's foreword, and Patty Reid, who works with Mario and has been one of my favorite people for years.

Lastly, I want to thank everyone who has appeared in the *The Wall Street Journal* My Ride column. At the time of this writing, there are nearly three hundred of you. Thank you for your time, thank you for your stories, thank you for your passion. Keep motoring! Drive safe.

A.J. Baime is the *New York Times* best-selling author of *The Accidental President: Harry S. Truman and the Four Months that Changed the World*. Previous books include *The Arsenal of Democracy: FDR, Detroit, and an Epic Quest to Arm an America at War* (2014) and *Go Like Hell: Ford, Ferrari, and Their Battle for Speed and Glory at Le Mans* (2009), both of which were optioned for major motion pictures. Baime is a longtime regular contributor to the *Wall Street Journal*, and his articles have also appeared in the *New York Times*, *Popular Science*, *Men's Journal*, and numerous other publications. He holds an M.A. in literature from New York University and currently lives in northern California. Visit A.J. at Facebook.com/ajbaime.